Mary Chamberlain was born in London in 1947 and spent her childhood there. After taking her degree in Politics from the University of Edinburgh and an M.Sc. in International Relations from the London School of Economics, she worked at the Foreign and Commonwealth Office and at the Richardson Institute for Conflict and Peace Research. In 1972 she left London to live in the Fens, where she taught Liberal Studies at the Norfolk College of Arts and Technology. While there, she wrote her first book, the highly acclaimed *Fenwomen: A Portrait of Women in an English Village*, published by Virago in 1975. In 1977 she returned to London, where she became senior lecturer in Cultural Studies at the London College of Printing until 1987. She is President of the Oral History Society and co-founder of the London History Workshop Centre. Author of *Old Wives' Tales* (Virago, 1981) and editor of *Writing Lives* (Virago, 1988), Mary Chamberlain now lives in Barbados with her husband and three children.

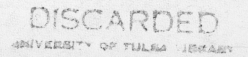

Mary Chamberlain

GROWING UP IN LAMBETH

VIRAGO

Published by VIRAGO PRESS Limited 1989
20–23 Mandela Street, Camden Town, London NW1 0HQ

A CIP Catalogue record is available
from the British Library

Typeset by Rowland Phototypesetting Limited
Bury St Edmunds, Suffolk
Printed in Great Britain by
Cox and Wyman Limited
Reading, Berks.

HQ1600
L6
C53
1989

Contents

For Peter and Alice

Acknowledgements

There are so many people to whom I owe deepest thanks for helping me with this book.

Perhaps those who contributed most to the making of the book were the women of Lambeth with whom I spoke. They gave me their time and, most importantly, their memories, allowing me to enter into their lives and their perceptions with an unfailing generosity and openness. I was always greeted with warmth and hospitality and spent many happy hours talking with them. I remember the following with particular affection, for I owe them a very special debt and my warmest thanks: Mrs Atkins, Jean Barker, Mrs Begum, Mary Boon, Jean Chandler, Mrs Chowdhury, Ann Connollon, Kathy Connolly, Wyn Cozens, Dolly Davey, Mrs Davies, Dolly Driscoll, Pat Dixon, Irene Gillings, Mrs Harden, Winnie Harris, Helen Hatch, Emmie Honey, Lucy Hayford, Faye Lightbourne, Maria Marengo, Dolly Mather, Kitty Moody, Polly Neal, Mrs Nessa, Mrs Noad, Betty Norman, Mary Perry, Emmie Perton, Rozanne Pizzy, Yvonne Plows, Gladys Reddington, Maggie Regan, Rose Regwell, Kath Savage, Mrs Sharp, Gracie Stack, Jackie Steer, Laura Stubbs, Lily Taylor, Rita Thanarii, Alida Thomas, Rose Tomkins, 'Bobby' Tyler, Mrs Young, Mrs West, Julie Williams. Without their contribution *Growing Up In Lambeth* would never have been written. In a very real sense this is their book.

But I was an observer and a historian and interpreted and located what they told me. For helping me with this I owe very special thanks to James Cornford, Peter Lane, Ann Oakley, Raphael Samuel and Jerry White, who read the book in its draft stage. They gave their precious time and expertise to read what I had written and offer valuable comments and suggestions.

Their advice and encouragement was deeply appreciated, although they should not be held responsible for its final form. I must also thank Ursula Owen at Virago for her support and editorial comments, and for her patience.

In addition, there were many others with whom I spoke who offered insights into the area, or who went out of their way to help me contact local people. For this, thanks are due to Roger Bagge, Nisha Chowdhury, Canon Clements, Freddie Lambert, Peter Lane, Father Vic McClean, Patricia Moberley, Ros Nash, Ethne Nightingale, Sarah Richards, Bernie Spain, Amanda Woolley and the Warden of the Kennington Park Day Centre. A particular mention must be made of Bernie Spain, who did so much to ensure that the Coin Street Community Development was successful but who, sadly and tragically, has since died. She is greatly missed by all who knew her, as a campaigner and as a friend.

I must also thank the Archivist of the Lambeth Archives, the staff of the Office of Population, Censuses and Surveys, the staff of the London Borough of Lambeth Research Department, of the Greater London Record Office and of the Inner London Education Authority Research Department, who shared with me their knowledge of the area and helped direct me to sources.

Acknowledgement must also be given to the Twenty-Seven Foundation, whose grant enabled me to carry out, and transcribe, oral material, to the Inner London Education Authority, who gave me sabbatical leave to continue my research, and to the London College of Printing, for giving me time off from my teaching duties to write. And I must thank my colleagues, for it was on their shoulders that the extra teaching load fell.

Those who have undertaken oral history research will know that great effort and skill is spent in transcribing the material and in this I was helped – with the aid of my Twenty-Seven Foundation Award – by Maureen Simpson, Jane Spratley and, in particular, Anita Walsh. To them I owe many thanks for undertaking the task of transcription so well.

Finally, though by no means least, I must thank, first, my

husband Peter Lane, who was the Labour Councillor for Bishop's Ward from 1971 to 1981. He had a particular knowledge of the area and helped, supported and encouraged me in many ways – practically, emotionally and intellectually by reading drafts, explaining, and patiently discussing ideas. Secondly, I must thank my parents, who, sometimes unwittingly, offered me insights into the area and whose reminiscences of their own childhood and youth I listened to and absorbed with relish.

In 1896 Maud Pember Reeves, a New Zealander, came to England with her civil servant husband. A social reformer and a feminist, she became concerned about the effects of poverty on the health of working-class families in London. In 1909, with other members of the Fabian Women's Group, she began an investigation into the daily budgets and daily lives of thirty-one working-class families living in Lambeth, on a weekly wage of about one pound. This investigation went on for four years, and in 1913 their findings were published as *Round About a Pound a Week*. This book was reprinted by Virago in 1979.

Returning to the area covered in *Round About a Pound a Week*, *Growing Up In Lambeth* records, chiefly through their own oral testimony, the lives of a group of Lambeth women, from the years between the two world wars to the present day.

The area covered in the two books stretches from Vauxhall in the west to Waterloo in the east, and south to the Elephant and Castle. The river Thames forms its northern boundary. The Houses of Parliament are on the opposite bank of the Thames.

The illustrations in this book are reproduced by courtesy of the following: London Borough of Lambeth Archives Department, Nos. 1, 5, 10 and 11; Greater London Photograph Library, Nos. 2, 3, 4, 6, 7, 8, 9 and 13; Lambeth Council, No. 12.

CHAPTER 1

The District

The year that Maud Pember Reeves arrived in London was the year that my grandmother, a seamstress, married my grandfather, a printer. The views have gone that my grandmother saw as she walked out in 1896, up through Waterloo, across Waterloo Bridge and into the Strand. Each bank, then, had huddled along its shores many of London's poor, and much of London's industry. The Palace of Westminster was a newish building; and the foundations of County Hall had not even been laid. St Paul's Cathedral still loomed over the City and dominated its skyline.

My grandparents set up a respectable house and reared six (surviving) children, the youngest of whom, born in 1913, was my mother. She went to school at the Elephant and Castle, in the same road as the London College of Printing, where, much later, I taught for ten years. They lived in Walworth, on the fringes of Kennington – where my grandmother finally died – and in Waterloo and Vauxhall. But my uncles and aunts would cross over the bridge to find their employment.

Further down the river my father, the youngest son of a docker, was born in 1912. A Bermondsey boy, he was born and bred in the shadow of Tower Bridge.

My parents married in 1940. With my father away in the war, my mother set up home, first, in my grandmother's house, until the bombing left them homeless and they sought refuge in the suburbs of South London, where I and my brothers grew up. Tales the family told were rooted in Southwark and Lambeth; it could not be otherwise, for our roots have been there since the 1800s. As a youngster I travelled to Town (as we called it) and would look, as my train crossed into Charing Cross, at its neighbouring bridge of Waterloo. It held, even then, a fascination, for it seemed to straddle my roots and my future.

I think of these things when I walk over Waterloo Bridge. I pass the South Bank arts complex – new when I was a student and discovering films other than those shown at the local Astoria, or music that came from an orchestra and not from the crackles of the Light programme on the family wireless (which was never switched off). That complex is now, in places, over thirty years old. But it is, more or less, my contemporary and so for me it never ages. On its site, a hundred years earlier, stood the Canterbury Docks, and the lead works, and the coal wharf and the brewery, and in their shadow lived its workers. They were standing when the Royal Waterloo Hospital for Women and Children, just south of the bridge, was opened. Now, having survived the bombings and the redevelopment, the Hospital is an American College.

Between the Hospital and the National Theatre runs Coin Street, site of a celebrated victory for community planning; here the people of Waterloo resisted, for a decade, the advances of the City, its wealth and its planners and have won for themselves the right to build homes. My husband was councillor here, for most of those years, fighting to get through the Waterloo District Plan which laid the groundwork for their success.

Beyond the roundabout, just before Waterloo Station reaches out, is St John's Church, where my great-grandfather married Ellen Banks on 12 April 1871. They, too, must have walked that bridge, and south again, through the narrow streets which still remain at the back of the station, filled with little terraced cottages built to house the porters at the old Covent Garden market. Those cottages remain, though most of those who live there now see them only as quaint and inconvenient. But there are a few who live there, newcomers and old, who fought hard in the Battle of Coin Street, to retain a bit of this past and to marshall it for the future.

The South-Western Railway Company bought up the land neighbouring Waterloo Station, in order to enlarge that terminal. In recompense, the company built accommodation for the tenants it had displaced. Stangate Buildings in Upper Marsh rehoused 290 people; Coronation Buildings in the South Lambeth Road rehoused 900, and Campbell Buildings (now demolished) stretched virtually from Westminster Bridge Road to Waterloo Road, and provided new accommodation for 1,460 people. Purpose-built tenements of 1903, they were a pride and joy, meticulously cared for by the tenants, and maintained by the landlords. But later they came to serve as vessels of containment and degradation to their tenants.

The South-Western Railway may have been the first to remould the area; it was not the last. Lambeth's housing 'problem' became a priority for the London County Council and its successors, the Greater London Council and the Borough of Lambeth, as it was for private philanthropists like Peabody, who founded the Peabody Trust. In 1913, when Maud Pember Reeves published *Round About a Pound a Week*, 38,816 people in Lambeth lived more than two to a room. In 1920, 20 per cent of the families who visited the Barley Mow Welfare Centre in this area lived in one room, and 30 per cent of those families who visited the centre regularly lived in one room.[1] Houses designed as single-family dwellings were occupied by several families and their lodgers. Space was let by the room, and the rooms occupied by a family were not always on the same floor, and not always interconnecting. The hall and the stairways were not only the means of access to a family's rooms, but an integral part of a family's living space. Self-contained units were rare.

Rooms were let, sub-let and traded as family fortunes rose and fell. When the rent could no longer be paid, families were thrown out on to the street. The houses were often infested and unsanitary. Despite what was called the 'Lambeth Policy' – of keeping houses under supervision and serving defect notices where necessary – few landlords cared or could afford to keep their property in good repair; they were secure in the knowledge that a less demanding tenant could always be found. The Policy had its greatest success in prevailing upon the larger landlords, such as the railway companies, the Duchy of Cornwall, or the Peabody, Guinness or Hayles and Walcot estates, to make improvements.

As you walk around the area near the refurbished Old Vic theatre in Waterloo Road, there are monuments to housing philanthropy, municipal and private 'buildings' – horizontal tenements – which stand still, the mellow brick of London still bearing the marks of the steam age and the city's pollution when the Old Cut, and Lower Marsh, and Upper Marsh – names which themselves evoke far more of the area's geological history – belched out unchecked the fumes and filth from the offensive trades which were carried on: Field's the fat melters and soap boilers, or Harris, Blackman and Sons, the tallow melters. None of the face-lifts of the City and West End here: the bricks remain black, the paintwork green, and the asphalt courtyards and balconies limit space and life as much as do the boards which cover the windows of the ground-floor dwellings.

York Road links the southern end of Waterloo Bridge with that of Westminster Bridge. County Hall and the Lying-In Hospital are all that remain of the pre-war York Road. The river frontage used to have wharfs and timber yards and potteries, and people. Now the complex of Shell International dominates not only York Road, but also its lowly neighbour, Belvedere Road. In 1938 there were thirty-four industrial firms and workplaces in Belvedere Road – the London County Council Tramways Department, six engineering works, one printer's and four plant machinery manufacturers, three brick-and-tile-makers, six wharfage storage firms and importers, one furniture-maker, two lead and metal smelters, one chandler, a large brewery, a builder's, a coal merchant's, a theatrical hat-maker's, various miscellaneous firms including one Investment Trust Company, as well as four pubs and five refreshment rooms . . . Now, it contains a car park, the Jubilee Gardens, the river walk, and the nomadic Australians who exchange and barter their mobile homes.

Westminster Bridge Road leads down from here, past what was once the old Canterbury, perhaps the most notorious music hall in South London, past the pubs and the shops which are now more likely to sell handbags and shoes than fruit and veg, past the homeless who coil, as they have always done, under the arches, or shuffle with the remnants of their home and life in bulging plastic bags, occasionally picking up casual trade in the market in Lower Marsh, finding shelter and pickings in Waterloo Station, or St John's; past the police station and the Methodist church, past Morley College – a living monument to Lilian Baylis – to St George's Circus, where five major streets converge.

St George's Roman Catholic Cathedral, where I was married one April, stands as if shunted along by the Circus. Once Gothic, war damage reduced its proportions and its colours. It looks solid enough now, but its cultural foundations in mid-Victorian Lambeth were precarious. My mother went to school opposite, in the convent run by the nuns of Notre Dame. And so did my grandmother, paying a penny a week for the rudiments of reading, writing, arithmetic and needlework.

Bethlehem Hospital, the notorious mental hospital known as Bedlam, stood opposite: the building now houses the Imperial War Museum, whose bellicose exterior does little to soften its earlier horrors, and whose interior, once behind the exhibition space, still remains as an unreconstructed memory of those times. My grandmother, and my mother, used two phrases to control their children. 'You're enough to try the patience of a saint', was one and the other, 'You'll drive me to Bedlam'. Here, where St George's and Bethlehem meet, was the embodiment of my childhood.

Some of the houses in St George's Road were built to house the nurses and doctors of Bethlehem Hospital. They still set the tone, as St George's Road spills over into West Square where Cabinet Ministers, and sometimes their mistresses, have and do set up house. For this is still within the call of the Division Bell. It is as if the combined presence of the parliamentarians, of Bedlam and the old Lambeth Workhouse in

Brook Drive and the relieving officer, the 'bun house' in Renfrew Road, still exert a presence, reminding its inhabitants of who defines and controls resisters and miscreants, and how . . .

That triangle between St George's Road and Kennington Road stands unique and apart from the rest of the area. Miraculously, much of it survived the devastating damage of the war. The old houses remain, some occupied by a single family, many multi-occupied. Within the infinite subtleties of English class, this was respectability. Indeed respectability was – and is – crucial; the Duchy of Cornwall and the Hayles and Walcot charities, who built here for the benefit of the 'poor and needy' remain large landlords controlling a heritage of decency through a heritage of tenancy. There are still streets and corners, angles and shadows which allude to this past. But this, too, may be changing as the Duchy begins to sell off its property to the new middle classes.

Over half the buildings in and around the Elephant and Castle, a few yards further south, were either destroyed or damaged beyond repair during the Second World War. The Elephant has been for the most part rebuilt, beyond recognition. The Department of Health and Social Security occupies one corner, opposite and above the shopping centre which now controls this central space. But the old South London Press building, surrounded still by a bomb site which doubles as a parking lot, and the old Spurgeon's Tabernacle with its fierce mock-classic exterior stand as images of the old Elephant, as monuments to absence. The London College of Printing now looms on another corner of that complex of cross roads, a shabby skyscraper from the sixties when building up provided instant answers. My office in that skyscraper over-looked the spot where my grandfather, in the 1920s, alighted from a tram and was knocked down and killed by a passing cyclist.

Behind the neighbouring façades of the College and the Tabernacle is another bomb site and parking lot – with some parking for cars and some for prefabs, the temporary expedient for the wartime homeless mocking time forty years on. It is here that Brook Drive, the backbone of this triangle of respect-ability, runs out of respect, divides into tributaries, a delta of despair. And the back of Spurgeon's Tabernacle, 1950s reconstruction, symbolises the two faces of the Elephant.

Kennington Lane leads down from the Elephant and up to Vauxhall Cross. Between Kennington Lane and the Lambeth Road there is another neighbourhood, or two. Off Lambeth Road is Lambeth Walk whose famous song and market sings no more in its new pedestrianised precinct.

The London County Council made it an 'action area'. The first major Improvement Scheme in Lambeth was around the China Walk area, where the houses rested too close and sometimes back to back. Those streets were demolished in the 1920s and replaced by LCC flats, horizontal tenements of discrete family units. It was followed through the 1920s and 1930s by similar schemes around Vauxhall, Waterloo and Kennington. And where the LCC failed, the war succeeded, for this area caught most of the bombs intended for Westmin-ster, just across the water. Scarcely a house or a street remains now that does not owe its origins to twentieth-century mu-nicipal planning; there are acres of estates built between the wars, and new estates.

Only 5.8 per cent of housing is owner-occupied; the rest is rented. Between 1913 and the present the local authority has virtually eliminated the smaller private landlord. Over 63 per cent of the housing stock is now owned by the council. The large private landlords, such as the Duchy of Cornwall, the railway companies and the various philanthropic trusts, account for another 27 per cent of accommodation. Only 2.55 per cent is owned by small landlords.[2] The prospect of council housing has been transformed from an aspiration into an expectation.

Between the wars, and particularly during the 1930s, unem-ployment was high, as local industry was subject to the fluctu-ations of a wider economy. But industry was rooted in the area, tied to its locality by transport and by the workforce. While employment fluctuated, the workplaces on the whole remained. Total change was difficult to envisage, and though the built environment must at times have confirmed pessimism, it also stood as a reminder of better times in the past and signified the possibility of better times to come. For all the instability of the period, it offered a certain constancy as well.

That constancy no longer exists. In the post-war reconstruction of the area, industry was given incentives to move, and many factories closed down or left. At the same time office development was encouraged. Within thirty years the industrial and economic composition of the Borough had changed drastically.

Since most of the industry and commerce was concentrated in North Lambeth, it was this part of the Borough which suffered the most marked changes. Between 1971 and 1981 Waterloo lost 52 per cent of its commercial floorspace and 30 per cent of its industrial floorspace, and Vauxhall lost 53 per cent of its industrial and commercial floorspace.[3] Between 1971 and 1979, in manufacturing and construction alone 16,540 jobs were lost – 45 per cent of the 1971 employment total.[4]

At the same time, in contrast, jobs in the office and service sectors rose. In particular, jobs in public administration rose by 43 per cent. Most of the change occurred and continues to occur in North Lambeth. Sixty-four per cent of employment in this area is now in office work, and much of that in public administration.[5] These office developments attract the new migrant worker, the commuter who daily invades from the suburbs and beyond. Few local people find employment there – save for the women who clean on the twilight shift between day and night. Once a major industrial area with local employment offered for local people by such household names as Myers', Marmite, Sarsons' and Doulton's, North Lambeth now offers little more than the menial tasks handed down from a service-based economy. There has been a marked diminution in the number of skilled workers living and working locally. Families were already moving out in the 1950s and 1960s, and between

1971 and 1981 the number of children under fifteen in the area halved, while the number of young people between the ages of sixteen and twenty-four increased by one-third. More and more of these young people were out of work.[6] Unemployment more than doubled between 1971 and 1981 and, among single women, it almost trebled.[7] It was nearly 40 per cent higher in 1981 than it was in 1931.

What were once local facilities now cater for the daily invasion of office workers from outside: it is the office workers' hours and needs that dictate the times and produce of shops, for example. The area, particularly around Waterloo and Vauxhall, is busy in the morning and evening rush hours, and in the lunch breaks, offering the illusion of a local life that has long since died.

When, in 1909, Maud Pember Reeves wished to explore and expose the daily lives of working-class women, North Lambeth was the area she chose as representative. She set out to argue the case that poverty and ill-health were the result not of ignorance or laziness but of insufficient income and inadequate housing. Put right the economic conditions in which the majority of the working class live, give those at the bottom of the social ladder a chance, and there would emerge a class of people who would be the equal of anybody. It was a social democratic ideal. Equal citizenship for all was a goal not only morally appropriate but capable of achievement. And in this, the role of the state as arbiter and catalyst was seen to be central, for neither private philanthropy nor private enterprise had the vision, funding or incentive capable of achieving this social revolution.

Originally, this book set out to chronicle change in North Lambeth and to compare the neighbourhood now with what it was in 1913. But as the story progressed that theme became more difficult to sustain, for a simple reason.

I was struck as I read and re-read Maud Pember Reeves at how worthy was her endeavour, and how dull. I was struck too by how much this sense permeated the lives of the women she described. Over and over again she refers to 'these steady people' 'these respectable men' with wives 'quiet and decent'. She describes their homes as 'monotonously and drearily decent', the street as 'quiet and desperately dull', with a 'dull aloofness' covering 'dreary acres – the same little two-storey house, with or without an inconceivably drearier basement'.

Although I was brought up in suburban London, the folklore of my childhood, rooted in this and its neighbouring area, seemed far from dull or dreary. My mother's family was highly respectable, too, and did not have to struggle to make ends meet, for my grandfather was 'in the print'. My father's family were less well provided for, for his father died early of pneumonocosis, from inhaling the dust from the corn wharves in which he worked. Industrial compensation was then un-heard of. Yet the stories from my parents and my grandmother were rich and lively, and full of laughter, however painful their origin. This was, they told me, the 'real' London.

They were also full of a meaning, which I could understand only later. Why was it important that one family served milk from the bottle, and not the jug? Or 'plonked' the food on the table, instead of arranging it 'decently' on the plate? Why was it that my grandmother took in my cousins, and my great-uncle Jack, so that 'dreary' little house was bursting with family? That my mother was never allowed to play in the street? What about the huge family gatherings at Christmas with the cousins from Poplar? Or my uncle's prize Alsatian whom my great-uncle Jack ruined, while my uncle was away, by walking her to the pub each evening?

All of these stories, and many more, are about family, about neighbourhood and about class. For those 'dreary' acres were far from 'monotonous', and far from monolithic. They were the battleground where a war of class and status was fought and defended. It mattered if you took in washing, visited the pawn shop, if shoes were unpolished and clothing torn. It mattered if you drank tea from a saucer, if the table was not laid, if the curtains were not washed weekly. It mattered because in those finer rituals and finer manners lay a definition of self, and a differentiation from the neighbourhood, a way of circumventing and resisting the threat of destitution which lurked forever round every corner of working-class neighbourhoods. My grandmother, and many, many like her, maintained payments on burial insurance, so that in old age they could feel safe from the threat of a pauper's funeral, sure of dying with dignity, secure from the attentions of the Poor Law which, long after it had gone, haunted the bleakest imaginings of the working class.

However poor their circumstances, however hard and tangled their lives, people are resourceful, and they are rarely willing victims. Where poverty is circumvented, culturally, and emotionally, if not economically, life becomes in part a pretence, but pretence is central to survival. However deep the deprivation, opportunities are found and made, whether in laughter or in dreams, whether in individual or collective choices.

I would like to believe that Maud Pember Reeves and her assistants were not insensitive to the inner life of working-class Lambeth. But Pember Reeves was a political campaigner and *Round About a Pound a Week* was a polemic. Though it may now be taken as a historical source, that was not its intention. Pember Reeves's purpose was to show that the families of the working classes were caring people and skilful managers of their limited resources. Pervading the book was the heavy hand of middle-class philanthropy and a political attitude which saw the working classes as a uniform whole and their values as pale reflections of middle-class mores.

Moreover, the women she talked to were from a particular constituency, drawn from those who attended the out-patient clinic of a 'well known lying-in hospital', which in 1909 would have represented only those women with the time, money and willingness to attend. Ante-natal and post-natal care were far from routine. Within that context, Pember Reeves and her assistants must have represented the authority of the state, to whose prying interference no family secret would be revealed.

As I interviewed women for this book I found I could not keep my analysis within the strait-jacket of comparison. These 'steady' people in fact manipulated their lives and displayed an ingenuity which far exceeded that required for thrift and frugality. Even thrift was more than a simple question of book-keeping. It was a refined evasion.

Growing Up In Lambeth, therefore, although inspired by Pember Reeves and informed by her work, is no longer a simple comparison between 'then and now'. Rather it is a conversation between the concerns of Pember Reeves and those of the historian, between the women who lived and live in North Lambeth – and between myself as an outsider and the 'real London' of my family.

This book is about the social contours of Lambeth's working class, about the material and economic contours which shaped them, and about the cultural environment which was shaped by them. It is about women growing up in Lambeth since 1913, their descriptions and ambitions, their subversions and move-ments. And, like *Round About a Pound a Week*, *Growing Up In Lambeth* is about survival – though its prescriptions for the future cannot now be so clear.

References
1. Barley Mow Welfare Centre, *13th Annual Report*, 1926/27.
2. London Borough of Lambeth, *1981 Census: Ward Profiles*, RM23, 1981.
3. London Borough of Lambeth, *Results of the 1978/79 Land Use and Employment Survey for Lambeth*, RM19.
4. Ibid.
5. Ibid.
6. Figures composited from *1981 Census: London Borough of Lambeth Ward Profiles*, RM23.
7. Unemployment Figures, Lambeth

	men	women	juveniles
1931	10.57%	7.2%	3.06%

(*London Statistics*, XXXVI)

1981   13.9%   12.5%   n/a   (*1981 Census*, RM23)

Unemployment Figures, Bishop's and Prince's Wards (Vauxhall and Waterloo)

	men	single women	married women	
1971	5.5%	3.0%	3.4%	
1981	13.2%	7.9%	4.0%	(*1981 Census*, RM23)

CHAPTER 2

Neighbours and the Neighbourhood

Should the man go into hospital or the workhouse infirmary, extraordinary kindness to the wife and children will be shown by the most stand-off neighbours, in order to keep the little household together until he is well again. A family who have lived for years in one street are recognised up and down the length of the street as people to be helped in time of trouble. Those respectable but very poor people live over a morass of such intolerable poverty that they unite instinctively to save those known to them from falling into it. A family which moves two miles away is completely lost to view. They never write, and there is no time and no money for visiting. Neighbours forget them. It was not mere personal liking which united them; it was a kind of mutual respect in the face of trouble.[1]

Between the wars, despite the Improvement Schemes, Lambeth's Medical Officer of Health in his Annual Reports commented year after year that 'there has been no marked change in the social conditions'. In 1935, for instance, out of 76,924 families in Lambeth, 3,881 were considered to be living in overcrowded conditions: nearly three-quarters of these – 2,724 – were living in tenement houses in North Lambeth, letting directly from the landlord or indirectly from another tenant.

Overcrowding necessarily blurred the distinctions between public and private life. Neighbours knew one another's business. Family noises and rows filtered through into the street. Within the neighbourhood of the house, how people slept, when they slept, where they slept, what work was done and taken in, which rooms were vacant, who was dirty, who was clean, who was healthy, who was sick, who was in work, who was without ... all of this was common knowledge. With shared hallways, stairs, doors and balconies, it was impossible to contain a family and maintain a discrete existence.

'My mother had the basement', recalled Lily White, who was born in Vauxhall in 1904,

> ... and we had a lady on the passage level. She had two rooms with a folding door. The dad was a nightworker on the trams and they only had one bed. The dad used to sleep in the bed in the daytime and when he went to work, mum and the three kids used to sleep in the bed. The one above that was Granny Hudson and her daughter, and our bed-rooms was right at the top. The living room and scullery was right down the bottom, and the two bedrooms was right at the top!

Overcrowding, equally, made for bad feelings. The points of contact and of sharing were too numerous to allow for harmony all the time. Who last cleaned the stairs, used the lavatory, used the wash-house: all were points of potential friction.

Violet Harris was born in Vauxhall in 1900. She married in 1917 and brought up her children in a variety of rooms in Kennington.

> I had to take the three little children right down to the damp, dark wash-house to do me bit of washing, so I could keep an eye on them. Everyone in the house used that wash-house. And very often you went after one where they never even emptied the copper out or tidied it up. And the woman in the basement used to buy these here beetroots, up the market. And she used to boil them in the copper and take them down the Walk [Lambeth Walk] on a Sunday morning to sell them.
>
> She'd boil them in the copper, and left it all red. And do you know what? She used to scoop them out the so-and-so

copper with a piss-pot. And she wouldn't wash that copper out. That was left for the next one. You couldn't complain. That wasn't much good. The landlord never lived near us, you know. And she'd just leave you one in the gob as look at you, you know? Oh, she was a tough customer. We had just to put up with that. Filthy, filthy woman.

Under such conditions it was necessary to generate ground-rules for survival, and it was these ground-rules which became the cultural heart of a neighbourhood. 'Standards' were of enormous importance. They could differ according to circumstances, but at base they forged the links within a network. Standards set the criteria for communal living, of trust, of help, exchange and co-operation. Standards were the means by which you assessed a neighbour, when neighbours lived within the home.

Standards determined honesty: at the most basic level, you had to be able to rely on your neighbours not to steal your possessions, at a time when few people had locks to their doors. You had to repay debts, a crucial ingredient in the ability to negotiate credit, whether from a landlord or a shopkeeper, a moneylender – or even a neighbour.

Day to day, there was a direct reliance on neighbours' willingness to co-operate, and their standards of cleanliness. This was particularly important to women, for it was they who had to negotiate over shared facilities, and they who were responsible for cleaning communal areas.

Molly Nelson was born in Drury Lane in 1901, but as a child moved to Waterloo, where she was brought up by an aunt. She married in 1920.

We knew what days we had to do the passage. After all, we walked in it as well as them. The stairs that went up to our room, we did those stairs ourselves and whoever was up at the top did those stairs. There was no argument. And if anybody was away, we just used to do the whole lot. Just mucked in.

Queenie Thomas, who was born in 1913 at the Elephant and Castle, recalled how:

> In our house there was sixteen people and we all used the one outside toilet with a flat wooden seat. Couldn't lift it up, you all had to sit on the seat regardless. But they was always kept nice, scrubbed white and clean. All take turns, once your week, my week, the next week . . .

Lodgers had to be as reliable, trustworthy and clean as the tenants from whom they sub-let. Where possible, therefore, lodgers were chosen from a circle of relatives or acquaintances: for example, a lodger might be the son or daughter of a neighbour.

Ada Terry was born in 1917 and brought up in and around Vauxhall.

> I can remember one lodger she [her mother] had there, he worked on a round, he had a van and used to go round to confectioners', delivering, and he'd take us with him on the van . . .
>
> [sings]
>
> > Our lodger's such a nice young man
> > A nice young man is he
> > So good, so kind
> > To all the family.
> > He's never going to leave us
> > Oh dear, oh dear, no
> > He's such a goody, goody man
> > Mama told me so.

Neighbourhood support was a powerful ally and a powerful incentive to conform to the principles of community, to standards in areas as fundamental as trust, as superficial – but potentially irksome and explosive – as cleanliness or noise. The willingness to help a neighbour with services or provisions, at the time of a birth or a death, say, or in periods of unemployment or economic stress, the willingness to intervene in domestic disputes, to shoulder temporary care for a neighbour's children, all of which had been shrewdly observed by Maud Pember Reeves, continued between the wars.

Kate East was born 'around 1900', and came as a young child from Walworth to the Elephant and Castle, where her mother took on the rental of a large nine-roomed house and sub-let it to tenants. Kate continued to live in the house after her marriage, and, like her mother, she rented out rooms there until very recently.

A person came to live here once, and she took one or two rooms at the top of the house. She'd been here a time, you know, then two or three times when she came down to pay me the rent she said, 'I've been looking for a place, Mrs East.' I thought to meself, it's funny keep saying that when she pays her rent, so I said, 'What's the idea? Ain't you satisfied?' So I said, 'Or is it the baby?' I suppose she thought perhaps I hadn't noticed. She said, 'Why, wouldn't you mind?' So I said, 'Well, I'm rather partial to children as long as you now how to look after them.' She was expecting, see. So she stayed.

She had it, then she had another one, twelve months after. Of course, I used to go up if she went out, if I heard a cry or the baby woke up, I'd go up and see to it. I looked after the baby when she went away to have the other one, then she had her veins done. She didn't think she'd go. I said, 'Well, if it's going to do any good, I'll look after the children.' Otherwise it meant him stopping away from work, see. I looked after the two of them.

Upholding standards was a passport to this society. Standards united and divided. They offered security for those who met and upheld them. They also discriminated against transgressors. Those who deviated from accepted standards were unlikely to receive neighbourhood support in their time of need.

Such perceived deviation may also explain, in some cases, why people were 'shopped' by their neighbours for defrauding the Board of Guardians. Of course, such 'shopping' also probably often occurred simply because of a personal grudge. In any case, it was seen as the ultimate repudiation of neighbourliness. Molly Nelson recalled with bitterness the time she was 'shopped'. Those in receipt of parish relief ('on the bun house') would have their benefit stopped if it was found that either partner had been working. But that was not all: stoppage was often accompanied by a prison sentence.

> My husband was on the bun house, and I had this job. Then when I went hopping I asked a friend next door, would she do the job while I was away. You was away five or six weeks then. Well, when I came home, somebody shopped me. Says Mrs Nelson's been drawing bun house money. Half a crown [12½p] a week. My poor husband got six months. That's doing a good turn, that is.

The neighbourhoods and communities of North Lambeth were carefully categorised as 'good' or 'bad', as much by the inhabitants as by police and other authorities. They took on a collective identity, a collective standard, internal and external, against which others were measured. A bad reputation – such as that enjoyed by Waxwell Terrace in the 1920s for 'vice and crime',[2] and housing 'all pros in back rooms, you know?' (Queenie Thomas) – may have become a badge of resistance for its inhabitants, against the authority of the police and, perhaps, against that of the more respectable neighbourhoods next door.

Fanny Abbott was born in Vauxhall in 1913. She and her brothers and sisters lived in the same house as their grandmother, a moneylender.

> Ada Lewis's lodging house, down the bottom of Lambeth [Walk]. It was a lodging house for women and that, naughty girls, down and outs. One day, there was all police down there. Of course, me nosey, I went down with my friends to have a look and I don't know if the woman was murdered or she done it, or she died or what, but they said 'They're

bringing the body out now.' I was enjoying myself, wasn't I? Till Mum found out. Wasn't supposed to go there. If we'd been somewhere and we shouldn't, you'd get a backhander, up to bed . . .

But a good reputation carried with it tangible advantages in employment opportunities, in credit facilities, and above all in terms of status.

Carrie Telford was born in 1912 and brought up in Roupell Street, in Waterloo, where she still lives. Her father was caretaker of the local school, a job which she inherited in her later years.

Roupell Street, Whittlesea Street, Thede Street, was three streets known as the white curtain streets of Lambeth. Supposed to be the posh part. You wouldn't see them standing at their doors talking in this street. But in the back streets, Ethelm Street, they used to call that 'Kill 'Em and Eat 'Em Street', well, you'd see all the women there with their arms folded, their sleeves rolled up, outside the doors jawing to one another, you know. But you didn't see that down this street, and we had to run past Ethelm Street because all the kids down there would hit us because we were in the posh street . . . There was pubs there and a man got murdered in one once so we called it 'Kill 'Em and Eat 'Em Street' ever since. There was a lot of stall-holders down there.

We weren't allowed to play in the street. My mother, and all the people in the street, wouldn't let their children play in the street: 'No, you're not going to play out here, you go to the park, go into the gardens and play.' Waterloo Church gardens.

They were very nice people lived here, ever so nice. There was two or three policemen down here, and there was a lot of church people. You had to get three references to get in the house, a vicar's reference, and your boss, and somebody that had known you a long time. And I don't think anybody ever owed rent.

For rent to be paid regularly, employment had to be regular. The main breadwinner had to have a 'good' job, while a 'good' address was in itself a reference. It was, moreover, a statement of pride when the opportunities for self-respect were limited. The popularity of LCC housing, of Peabody buildings and the Duchy property, of the 'railway' accommodation of Campbell Buildings and the 'police' accommodation of Edward Henry House had as much to do with status as with the facilities they offered. Many of the regulations in this type of accommodation were strictly enforced and restricted precisely that form of communal living to which most families in other accommodation were used – Peabody did not allow talking on the communal staircases, for instance, and attempted to regulate children's noise – and yet few women were prepared to resist. Indeed, they assumed responsibilities far beyond those required, such as polishing the dustbin lids, and whitening the communal stairs, generating new and personal symbols of status.

Maude Springer was born in Waterloo in 1900. She married in 1919 and a few years later she and her husband managed to find a place in Campbell Buildings.

It was a hard job to get in Campbell Buildings . . . but there's always ways and means . . . I don't know if I like the word 'key money'. I like to think it's a little gift rather than key money. You never paid much rent. And I was proud to think I lived in Campbell Buildings. They were lovely rooms. Lovely. I had two rooms, one bedroom, one dining room and you had like a kind of scullery . . . They used to polish the dustbin lids. You could have made your face up in them. Honestly, it was a treat to go up there and outside every door was that little patch of white. Every morning. Pure white. And the knockers were polished and everything. They had three caretakers there. And they would check who cleaned the stairs. We used to take it in turns. You could have eaten off the stairs.

Such symbols were statements about stability and security. They were not necessarily statements about class division.

Notions of neighbourliness and mutual aid could not be separated from the circumstances of working-class lives, lived against the backdrop of the street.

Many local people, like the costers in the market, made a regular official living out of the street. Nellie Brown, for instance, who was born in Waterloo in 1902, married a man who had a shoe stall in Lambeth Walk. She described her fellow stall-holders.

I'm not going to say they didn't quarrel at times because that's natural, they did. If one sold what the other one was selling, there would be an argument. Or if someone took your pitch. But if there was any hard trouble or anything, they would always help each other. They'd all muck in.

Some would make a less official living. Queenie Thomas's father was a policeman, and she subsequently married a bookmaker.

Of course, in them days, they used to have to bet in the streets. It wasn't legal and he used to stand in the street see, so therefore, they'd have a pitch with a look-out. There was one man used to take the money and then there'd be two or three look-outs, looking for the police.

Listen, the police used to come along and take a backhander. They knew it was going on, couldn't stop it, people liked a bet. Then now and again they used to take them in. They used to come round and tell them and say 'Look, we want a man tomorrow.' Well, they wouldn't send up anybody that had been done too many times, you know what I mean? Went on all the time.

My husband got caught a couple of times, but he never went inside. They used to run in one house, over the garden walls. They always got somewhere where there was an alley. You know Cleaver Square? Well, they used to stand round there, there's a couple of alleyways there, and they knew the old people who lived there and the big bookmaker would give them, say, about ten bob [50p] or a pound to let them stand in the doorway. They used to stand there and then get away out of the back, over the garden wall, see?

The street had the potential of offering some form of living to the unemployed. There was casual selling – of beetroots, perhaps, or tarry blocks, or firewood which could be scrounged and therefore required no capital outlay; and there was begging. Kitty Barnet was born in 1910 in Kennington. Part of her childhood was spent in the workhouse, but at other times,

My father, he had these eight kids, after the First World War, he took out a barrel organ and he had right across the front 'Wife and Eight Children to Support'.

In many cases, it was difficult to discern where begging stopped and entertainment began, as Lily White described:

My dad used to have a concertina, he used to go busking. And then when I was older, I used to go over there and hold the cap out, you know? His cap, off his head. I'd stand there and they'd be throwing their ha'pennies in, yeah, and pennies. But we used to get tanners over in Piccadilly.

Street entertainment was one attempt to make a living when none else was offered. Rene Grant was born in Kennington in 1910.

My husband was in the building trade in the hungry thirties. Couldn't get a job anywhere. So he and me brother-in-law picked up a load of shuttering, what they used to do the concrete with. Saw it up and chop it, get a barrow from Keens. They used to let barrows out all over Lambeth, 4*d.* [2p] a day. Then he used to go round the streets 'Firewood, oh! Firewood, oh!' Ha'penny a bowlful. One day, they couldn't get a customer so Bill turned round and said 'I'd get more bloody money', he said, 'if I was singing', he said. 'Well, go on then, have a go.' And he did, he had a good voice, Bill, he started singing. Well, everybody was chucking pennies out the window to him.

It was a thin line which separated the supplier from the consumer. At any point, anyone could be forced on to the streets to earn a living from their wits, to reverse the role from spectator to performer. Even for those lucky enough to be in regular work, survival depended on a close relationship with the street and its surroundings.

For the inhabitants of overcrowded homes, public facilities provided essential extra space. Lily White remembered how

> Saturday night, my mum used to send my dad to the pictures so she could bath us all, when we were kids. 'Go on, off to the pictures', she used to go . . .

The pubs provided extra room, particularly in the evening when there was little space at home for the parents to sit – a circumstance which was, sometimes, used to advantage by the children. Sal Beckford was born in Vauxhall in 1920.

> We could stay out nearly all night [then]. My mum and dad used to be up the Queen, the Queen's Head. We'd be staying out all night.

They also offered a temporary refuge from home life. Although some women were reticent about going into pubs, many used them regularly. Rose Parker was born in 1919 in Vauxhall.

> Monday was a day out for the women. Mondays was my mother's washing day. My mum's up the pub. We're at school, they're out. Well, when they'd had enough, they'd come home singing. She'd take them all in our kitchen, our back kitchen and we had a mangle, you know? A wringer. So they'd all be singing and there's someone'll say, 'Oh, turn the organ, turn the organ!' and there they'd be singing with the wringer going, you could hear the rollers going. And then when I put my head in the door, come home from school, you know, four o'clock, 'What are you doing?' I said, 'I've come home from school.' 'Out and play, out and play.' Because they was all singing. Wouldn't have us in there. My mother's boozing day, that was.

My mother was only ever going to have one, but she'd always stop, you know. 'I won't be long.' I said, 'I'll tell Dad when he comes home.' 'I'll kill you if you do', she used to say. My mum didn't dare tell him – though I think my father was a bit frightened of my mother, you know?

He was a butcher. But Mondays, he dreaded Mondays because he had to stay behind and scrub up, you know. They never done it over the weekend, so Monday was a slack day and he'd have to scrub up. When he come home he was really whacked out and I used to have to do his old smock. Oh, they was heavy smocks in them days, woolly, you know, them flannel smocks. And he stunk of meat, but when he used to come home, he used to say 'She all right?' I'd say 'Oh no, don't wake her, Dad, she's been up the pub.' Oh then, sometimes, he'd lose his temper, then it was a fight.

She was thick-set. Thick-set. I can see her now. She loved her half pint, my mum, she did. I used to have to go and get it, she'd say, 'Put it behind the mangle', so Dad wouldn't see it.

Fights were commonplace in the street, as the tensions of poverty and overcrowding were brought out to be aired – often in a pub, as drink would unwind tongues and tensions. Violet Harris never forgets the time when:

> there was a man and a woman coming down through the street, and this pub. He's walloping his wife. Oh, he knocked her down. She got up to have a go at him. Down she went again! And this man, behind, he give this husband one smashing blow in the clock and she's got up and she's giving him 'Bloody –, you leave him, sunshine, alone. That's my old man!' And she's got big black eyes!

The home was brought out to the street in other ways – Lambeth Baths, for instance, at the bottom of Lambeth Walk, was used for bathing and washing clothes, when so few had space for washing clothes, and even fewer, bathrooms. Although 'that was a luxury to go to Lambeth Baths. That cost three ha'pence or tuppence [about 1p].' The 'bagwash' in Oakley Street offered a slightly superior facility. Maude Springer was married to a local baker.

> Everybody took bagwash and we had a bagwash shop in Oakley Street, which is now Baylis Road and I think, if I remember rightly, it was 30 lb. 3s. [15p]. You all lined up of a morning, Monday morning, with your big bag of washing and you called for it Tuesday.

Many bakers, including Maude's, would open their ovens on a Sunday for the family joint to be roasted.

> We used to take people's dinners on Sunday. They used to fetch their dinners in a dish. We used to charge 4d. [2p]. That was for every Sunday. We used to put a tin number in one of the potatoes on the dish and then give you the same number that corresponded with that, so you couldn't argue that that bit of beef was bigger than yours. It was a sight to see Sundays, people taking their joint and bringing it home. But it was hard work, really, you had to clean up the bakehouse afterwards, the grease that was coming out the dishes.

A choice of commercial entertainment was offered in a range of local theatres, music halls and cinemas, although by the 1930s the cinema had become increasingly the preserve of the young, and of women. According to *The New Survey*, 70 per cent of the weekly audience consisted of girls and women. The cinema and music hall were popular and cheap. Sal Beckford told how,

> My dad used to say to my mother, 'Where you been today, love?' 'Oh, I went down Draper Street and done a bit of shopping.' Or he'd say 'Ain't you been out today?' 'Well, I been busy, Jack.' 'Oh well, we'll have a bit of tea and we'll go over to the old South', the old South London, in London Road, where they did turns and things.

The South London, the Surrey in Blackfriars Road, the Gattis in Westminster Bridge Road and the Canterbury, near the arches in Lower Marsh, were former music halls. By the period between the wars Gattis and the Canterbury were also showing films as part of their variety, with turns before and during the programme, in which the audience, borrowing the conventions of the music hall and pub entertainment, expressed their approval or disapproval through direct participation. Ada Terry recalled:

> The old Gattis and the Canterbury, they were really sounding grounds. If anyone went up the Gattis and got a few claps you could always bet they'd turn out to be stars.
>
> The Gattis used to be like – there was a pit, then there was a balcony all the way round, that was the tuppence ha'pennies, downstairs was thruppence. They used to call it the bug hutch. They had a stage, and the bloke used to sit in the pit playing, same old bloody tunes every time. Never mattered what was on. They used to sit on the side, eating, then pelt them. Every time you went to Gattis you had to get underneath, otherwise you'd be smothered. The Canterbury was more sedate. They couldn't throw anything at the stage there, because the stage was too far away.

The Old Vic attempted to encourage an appreciation of more 'cultured' entertainment, but, as Carrie Telford observed:

> We used to go to the Old Vic and we used to go up in the gallery of a Saturday afternoon. I don't know if we paid a ha'penny or a penny, but when you come out you got an orange and a bag of sweets. They didn't give them to you while you were there because of making a mess, you got it when you come out, see. And that was to teach you to learn to like ballet and opera and all that, see, when you were young. You went because you got a bag of sweets and an orange!

In the post-war reconstruction of North Lambeth, shopping precincts and cultural complexes were planned and built. They were symbols of the glory and hope of the post-war world. Class, in the optimism and affluence of the 1950s was thought no longer to exist. The class war, Harold Macmillan proclaimed, was over. Class had been restructured: socially by Beveridge's rationalisations of social inequality; geographically by the location of industry and housing beyond the city boundary; economically by the affluence which promised to characterise post-war Britain; and culturally by the growth of mass and centralised entertainment, the cinema, the radio and television.

There was to be no return to the messiness which had characterised class-torn pre-war Britain. Class itself could no longer be located, and should not be located, within its traditional, visible boundaries. The identification of class with place, of (for example) fixing the urban poor within the boundaries of streets, in a local cultural milieu, was no longer considered desirable or relevant. Although the new housing in the inner city was constrained by space, its form, nevertheless, was as different from that of the past as it was possible to be.

The culture that had depended on the street no longer existed. There was, therefore, no need for streets. Homes could be built vertically, and separated by open space. With no working-class culture, with the decline of working-class communities, housing need only be functional.

But if town planning attempted to reconstruct the built environment on the assumption that class no longer existed, or should exist (an assumption that was, in itself, heavily class-determined), it also planned on the assumption of specific gender roles.

Men worked and women stayed at home. Work and home were separated, and new homes, compact, easy-to-run, labour-saving, were to fulfil all the 'housewife's' dreams. Gone was the old notion of 'extended' family, replaced by that of the 'nuclear' family. The planners, in their designs of homes, estates and neighbourhoods, built on these assumptions. Domestic and industrial planning was both cause and effect. Contemporary architecture and planning were to be, above all, functional. Men and women had specific functions; the nuclear family had a function; work was a function. Function was rational and could, therefore, be planned. The kitchen could be planned and was as suited to time and motion studies as the factory. Good planning and labour-saving devices meant efficiency, which the post-war reconstruction of the housewife 'demanded'.

With the reconstruction of the home went the dismantling of the neighbourhood; and with the reconstruction of the inner-city went the destruction of locality.

Council housing is now the form of housing occupied by the majority of the people of North Lambeth. The council blocks, and the people within them, and their life-styles, are well established.

In the early days of council housing, it was thought necessary to appoint estate supervisors. The supervisor was a figure borrowed from the philanthropic housing trusts, a gatekeeper between tenant and landlord, responsible for maintaining philanthropic mores – and often for allocating property. The supervisors were not above corruption. 'Dropsy. Little dropsy,' said Gladys Harman. 'Yeah, it was all dropsy. You had to drop two bob [10p] or half a crown [12½p] to get in anywhere.' Their presence was often a mixed blessing, and they tend to be missed after their departure, but resented where they remain.

Judy Chalmers was born at the Elephant and Castle in 1937. The road she lived in was demolished after the war, and the family was rehoused in a newly built council flat in Waterloo.

This house was sort of the élite and then all of a sudden that seemed to go a bit downhill. Well, it seemed like the flats were going downhill fast . . . I think it was the people coming in mainly, plus the fact that we used to have a rent man knocking at the door so he knew everybody and if you hadn't done the stairs he would tell. He wouldn't say, 'You've got to get out', he'd tell you or you'd do it the day before he came. But then they stopped that. You started paying in the post office so there was nobody to keep an eye on you. I think this happened about ten years ago. So consequently nobody

seemed to bother and then new tenants came in that wasn't
particularly fussy, they was just pleased enough to get a place
but they wasn't fussy about the exterior and things just went
from bad to worse. It was the first block to go up in this area
after the war. They actually built it to rehouse the people
from the Festival of Britain site, so that would be 1951, but it
was completed about 1948 because they had to build it, put
the people in it, then clear that site. That's why all of them
went in together. They were all neighbours in Tennison
Street and all around, all those little rows of houses . . . Now
they've upgraded S—— House. Last time I looked at there I
think they were looking better than we was and yet they was
always, 'Look, don't go over there', you know. It was older
than this one.

We was always the élite, though you was nearer the
market and you'd got that much more rubbish. There was
less bigger families and all. Not like S—— where you've got
people with about eight kids, and much more mobility,
people coming and going more. That was always more of a
problem than our block. It seemed to us on the other side of
the road, always seemed that much more of a problem,
larger families. Now, we've had a few tenants move over
from S——. We've had a proportion of Philippines, nice
people, but nothing in common with the rest of the block . . .

The departure of the supervisors from council accommodation is not to blame for the decline in the fabric and conditions of
the flats. The benefactors of the philanthropic trusts had little
faith in the ability of the working classes to maintain their
surroundings, yet, with or without supervisors, until recent
times internal standards would have determined that the flats be
pleasant places in which to live. The generations who now, for
the most part, inhabit the flats were born and reared in a
different epoch and ambience where such external and communal standards have little force.

The structure of the buildings themselves enforced an
individualism, established discrete units in which, it was

believed, the working classes could be morally improved, for too much communality bred immorality. Ironically, those discrete units in themselves have helped create a generation which sees survival in terms not of communality but of self-interest. Each family, each unit, survives as best it can. Improvement lies in home décor and, ultimately, home purchase.

In some cases, however, the flat-dwellers have created their own networks, whether through organised tenants' associations or more informally. Accounts of these echo some of the stories of neighbourhood living between the wars – with its advantages and disadvantages.

Deirdre Patel was born in Ireland in 1952, but emigrated to England and settled in North Lambeth when she was sixteen. She married a Kenyan Asian and had two children by him, but the marriage subsequently broke up. She spent a year in bed and breakfast accommodation, then was rehoused in a flat in Kennington. She spoke warmly of her neighbour.

> I go out early morning cleaning, go out for me kids, and for me home, because I like them to have things. I don't get nothing from their dad. My neighbour's got the key, the lady on my floor. She's really good, she is. Auntie, we call her. Coloured lady. She's about seventy-three, but she's got a heart of gold, you'd never believe it, you know? If I ever go out, she'll keep it free.

Jackie Ball was born in 1950 and has one child. She was rehoused on a council estate in Vauxhall about twelve years ago, when her daughter was three.

> I didn't know anybody and was absolutely appalled because I'd never lived in council flats at all prior to that. I was amazed at how everybody knew everybody else's business. They were really thick with one another, really friendly, and then when they fell out, hollered each other's business all across the balconies when they had an argument, you know. You got to know everybody's business that way, even if you weren't involved with them at all.

Family networks are still a vital means of support. Karen West, a single parent with two children, described her family situation.

I had a little boy by my first husband and the girl. But that marriage never really worked out because he was one for motor bikes and he liked getting in a lot of gangs and trouble and he used to stay away at weekends so that never really worked out.

I was round my mum and dad's a lot. I could never cope . . . I was living with my mum and dad when we first got married and we only had her and my mum and dad could never really get on with my first husband and that. We was always arguing and he kept walking out so in the end I went down to the council and that and said I need a flat. And I waited for about a year or so and my mum and dad got their electric cut off so we was all up my brother's and his wife's, and then I finally got my flat, my mum and dad moved back down with me till they got sorted out and then my brother got evicted out, so I had a whole house full and my husband came back for a while but it never worked out and when the family finally did move back here my husband come back and we give it a long good try but he changed for a little while and then he went back to his own ways, you know? He never washed, his hands were always greasy and that from motor bikes and he started building a motor bike indoors and it wasn't very nice with the kids, and we had a little Alsatian puppy and when I said I wanted him to go, the bike was still in the passage, so I couldn't leave the kids there but I couldn't very well bring the puppy out. I was round my mum's one Friday night with the kids and when I got home the next day there was sick on the floor from the puppy so on the Monday I phoned my solicitor and told her, and he moved out in the end. Took the puppy with him because I couldn't afford to keep the puppy as well . . .

For the poor, informal support remains necessary for survival. But the demographic changes which have taken place within the area are leading to different life patterns. Extended families are often dispersed, leaving the old, and the young, isolated with only neighbours to call on for support. Neighbours can and do help out, in unofficial baby-minding, lending money or goods. But they cannot be expected, nor is it demanded, to shoulder greater burdens of support.

For many of the newcomers to the area there is an isolation not just from family, but also from the wider community. For instance, many Bengali women are separated from their neighbours by language, culture and creed. Mrs Chowdhury described how:

I came to England twenty years ago, from Bangladesh. I was fifteen years old. I came with my husband – we had just got married, when I was fourteen years and three months. My parents had arranged my marriage – I had never seen my husband because he was in England. Thirty years in England.

I felt very bad, odd, sad. I knew nobody. Very few Bengalis. No English. I spoke no English – I learnt when the children went to school and I went to English classes. At first, my husband bought everything. I didn't go out much, once a week. At that time, nobody friends much. But the English, then, were very friendly, all the time helpful, ladies and men, even policemen. When I came it was very cold, snowing. A policeman comes and talks. I can't understand and he held my hand, and pointed to go in. Now it is different. Everything change.

I have lived in Lambeth for twenty years, in a council house which my husband is now buying. He works for British Rail. It is very different from Bangladesh! I was twenty-one when my first child was born, and now have three children of fifteen, nine and seven years. Two boys and one girl, all born in England. I now go out, shop. But I don't go out after six – men can go, but not women. I feel unsafe. I take them out at the weekend, but not the weekday. Especially my children not going out.

And Mrs Begum:

I am twenty-eight and have been here nearly eight years. I came with my husband – I was married at fourteen. After a girl gets her period, then parents worried about her getting married. My parents arranged my marriage. I didn't know my husband, though we were distant relatives. He is twenty years old than me. I now have three sons of eleven, six and a half and two and a half.

But no family, no friends when I came and very upset. I spoke very little English. No English, no friends. It was a big problem. My son was two years and two months, he liked to play but I knew nobody. Sometimes, I cried. Now, my neighbours are very good and I talk with them. When my flat flooded, then the neighbours helped.

The children come home from school complaining of names, 'They called me a Paki, why?' We like everybody and I explain our religious way, that in Moslem everybody is a brother. I say, 'Don't say anything back to them.'

However, the Bengali community, like some other ethnic groups, has created its own centres, family centres where the mothers learn English while the children learn Bengali, maintaining an identity while striving for some form of cultural co-operation.

With the demise of the street as the creative force in the community, it seems that leisure has been stripped of its spontaneity. The trend towards centralisation of entertainment was boosted throughout the war, not only by the continuing popularity of the cinema, but also by the growing popularity of radio. The trend was further reinforced by the advent of television. As the sales and rentals of television sets grew in the 1950s and 1960s, cinema attendances dropped. Many of Lambeth's cinemas closed down; some remained as buildings only and, as the national 'mass culture' companies moved increasingly into leisure, were converted, like the Granada in the Kennington Road, to bingo halls.

Maggie Thorpe, who was born in 1957, lives in Vauxhall with her husband and young family. She says:

It's boring really round here no, like, social, night life. If you want night life, you've got to go over the west end or something. We don't go out much. We'd rather sort of sit indoors and, you know, he plays his records and I watch the telly and do things. But he used to, like when he was single, he used to be over there but I never used to bother. Like, I only go out if there's parties to go to, or if we decide to go out. But he don't drive. Can't afford a car.

But while television may be ubiquitous, spontaneous entertainment still exists. Much of the interwar entertainment was, simply, private. And still is. People still have parties, or go to the pub with friends. But in addition a range of community-based entertainment has developed in recent years. Many tenants' associations, for instance, have either got, or are agitating for, a hall in which to hold meetings and to provide a central and social meeting place:

Debbie Stebbings lives with her boy-friend and her daughter in one of the post-war tower blocks in Kennington. She was born in 1956 and was brought up by her mother who ran an off-licence. The skills she learnt at her mother's knee now come in handy; 'Very active, we are. We've got a building, I'm the secretary, I've been to court twice and got the drinks licence and the gambling licence.'

Others organise youth clubs or mothers' and toddlers' clubs. The growth of community organisations has offered not only a political outlet but also a social one, and many community associations see as central to their role the provision of a range of clubs and courses, from yoga to dance to womens' health groups.

But leisure and entertainment have ceased to be street-wise. After dark, indeed, the streets appear dead. This alienation from the locality, which community groups can only partially redress, in a subtle form of deprivation. It creates a sense of rootlessness.

References
1. Maud Pember Reeves, *Round About a Pound a Week*.
2. *New Survey of London Life and Labour*, 1934.

CHAPTER 3

Growing Up

Questions are often asked as to how these children amuse themselves ... As far as close observation could discover, they seemed to spend their play time – the boys shrilly shouting and running in the streets, and the girls minding the baby and looking on ... Girls sometimes pooled their babies and did a little skipping, shouting severe orders as they did so to the unhappy infants ... The pathways were full of hatless girls and babies who looked on with interest and envy.

In holiday time elder brothers or sisters sometimes organise a party to Kennington Park or one of the open spaces near by, and the grass becomes a shrieking mass of children, from twelve or thirteen years downwards. The weary mother gives them bread and margarine in a piece of newspaper ... On Bank Holiday these children are taken by their parents to the nearest park. The father strolls off, the mother and children sit on the grass. Nobody talks. There is scolding and crying and laughing and shouting, and there is a dreary staring silence – never conversation.[1]

What has it been like for children to grow up in Lambeth between the First World War and now? In particular, what has it been like for girls?

Between the wars, most working-class children in North Lambeth were expected to contribute, from an early age, to the economy of the family. These contributions were made either through money or goods, or through help in the home. The child's labour was in many instances crucial to the economic survival of the family.

Ada Terry was born in Vauxhall in 1917, one of eight children of a waterside labourer.

When I was about nine my aunt said, 'Why don't you send her over the other side, for some stale bread?' So I went.

It was a little, very high-class bakery, you know, sold cakes and that, used to sell these lovely sandwiches. Well then, the next time I took my young sister with me. We used to get up at four o'clock in the morning, go over from Kennington, all along the Albert Embankment, over Westminster Bridge, through part of St James's Park, up the Duke of York steps, when we landed at this here Jermyn Street, right opposite the Haymarket Theatre and up the side of Her Majesty's Theatre. And there we'd wait and all the other kids would come up, you know? We were always number one there, we made sure of that. And about eight o'clock this woman used to open.

On one occasion she said to me ''ere,' she said, 'now you look a sensible girl,' she said, and she said, 'you look about the oldest here' – they were quite young some of them, you know, 'you'll have to keep these children quiet and keep quiet yourself,' she said, 'because I'll have to stop serving you because the people, residents, have been complaining.' Well, of course, they was all very well-off people that lived round about there. I said, 'Oh, I know, lady, if you like I'll keep them quiet. Tell them little stories. The next morning when she opened up the shop I was number one in, of course, and she said 'You've been a very good girl. Have you been telling them some stories?' And I said, 'Yes'. 'You can have a ham bone.' Lovely ham, you know, off the bone. There was quite a lot of ham on it and my dad had a lovely tea off of it and we had some as well. But that's how I continued to go over, doing that, till I was fourteen and then my sister took over.

Lily White was born in 1904 in Vauxhall. She came from a family of nine.

Each day you went round a different butcher's and you bought three pennorth of giblets. Now most people, old people, know what a giblet stew is. It's made you see with all the giblets. You'd get a bag full for thruppence . . .

For the mothers, errands such as these were crucial: they helped expand the resources of a limited budget. But they were also time-consuming and had to be undertaken at inconvenient hours in the early morning, or in the evening, precisely at the time when young children's demands – and often their husbands' too – would be at their greatest. Sending the older children out on errands was not only practical for the domestic account, but got them out of the house, and out from under their mother's feet, at a time when such space and time were vitally needed. Clearly, for the children, such 'forages' were an adventure, as Ada Terry recalled:

Very often we'd be sitting there up on the window looking into the bakehouse, we used to lean to keep warm, and these well-off men, they'd been to these clubs and that, high hats on, you know – we used to call them 'toffs' – and one toff came up to us. 'Come on kids, have a scramble!' And you know – we all, we had no knickers, no nothing on underneath, you know? So poor. We used to pin, safety pin in between our, you know – he'd get these handfuls of silver out and 'Here you are!' Fling them all up in the air and we'd be toiling and scrambling and showing everything, you know, to grab, and we used to take it home to Mum. Never used to get nothing back, got none the more for that!

Fanny Abbott was born in 1913, the daughter of a coal delivery man.

When it was Derby Day we used to wait at the Horns [Kennington] for them to come back on the buses. In those days it was open-topped buses and all the winners . . . we'd say 'Throw out your mouldies!' Crowds of us kids, and they used to throw all the pennies off the top of the bus.

When were you allowed to join in? When did you have to share? When could you keep those gains for yourself? Fanny Abbott described the time when:

The man used to come round with 'Fine, large shrimps, winkles and watercress'. That's a Sunday. When we finished, they used to throw the blooming winkles in the gutter or in the street. So us kids, we'd say, 'See how many winkles you can find.' We're looking in the kerb for all the winkles that the people had thrown out after Sunday tea. Eventually, I found a shilling [5p] while we were picking the winkles. I went indoors and I said 'Look what I've found, Mum.' My mother's face, it all lit up. 'That's good,' she said. She only had 30*s*. [£1.50] a week then to bring us all up on.

But a contrasting story was told by Queenie Thomas.

Well, you were brought up honest. My mum had eight of us but – I got change of a pound once instead of a ten shilling note [50p] and my mum made me go straight back with the extra change. And I thought she'd be pleased and she said 'Don't you ever do that, you know, you knew it was wrong.'

For children, 'finders keepers' must have been a confusing moral guide. But no less so for their mothers. There was a utilitarian guideline. If the money could be clearly identified, then it had to be returned, especially if its legitimate owner was a local shopkeeper with whom maintaining good relations was an absolute priority. And yet such a guideline was framed on the margin of legality, of fine negotiations with those in positions of authority or power, the relieving officer, the means test man, the landlord, the tally man or the pawnbroker.

Children, and girls in particular, were often brought in to mediate between, for instance, the rent man and their mother, in the hope that a steely rent collector would be less hard on a child than on her mother. Delaying the rent was often necessary. It bought time. Ada Terry described how:

When my mother was hard up and couldn't pay her rent, she used to say 'Stop here. The rent man'll be here in a minute. Tell him I ain't got the rent. Can't afford the rent. You all right? I'll be behind the door.' And when they came along, you'd say, 'Mummy can't pay her rent. She told me to tell you.'

For many mothers, life was lived on a knife edge and their children were acutely aware of how tight money was and how any money would be welcomed and, conversely, how much the loss of any part of the family budget affected the arithmetic of survival.

Rose Parker was born in Vauxhall in 1919, the eldest of eleven surviving children.

I was the eldest, course, I had to do everything, you know? Get all the errands and she (mother) give me sixpence [2½p] to go and get a couple of loaves. And I'm going along, devil-may-care, and I drop the sixpence down an airey [area]. I could see the sixpence down there, but I couldn't get to it. It was an empty airey.

I wouldn't go home. So I'm sitting on the doorstep and it's getting a bit dark, and a policeman come along. So he said, 'Shouldn't you be home?' So I said, 'I can't go home.' He said, 'Can't go home, why?' I said, 'My mum's going to kill me.' He said, 'Whatever for?' I said, 'I've dropped sixpence down there.' He said, 'Well, come on, where d'you live?' I wouldn't tell him. I says, 'No, no, I'm not going home. I know my mum'll kill me.'

Well, somebody come through Lambeth Walk and they said, 'Oh, she lives just round the corner.' So he took me. My mum comes to the door and she seen me with the policeman. And she said, 'Don't fetch her here, I'll kill her.' So he said, 'Look, afore you start, she's lost the sixpence you sent her for bread.' So she said, 'Yes, and she hasn't been here since, no bread or nothing.' She said, 'She won't come in here, I'll kill her.'

The strain of poverty, of having to perform, at every meal, the miracle of the loaves and fishes, understandably exhausted patience. There was little room to ponder the difference between wilfully squandering sixpence and accidentally losing it. They had the same effect, and neither should have been allowed to happen. Girls, above all, should have been aware of this.

Discipline was more often than not meted out by the mother – for she was the parent with whom the children spent most time. And discipline tended to be sharp and perfunctory. Indeed, it must often have appeared erratic.

> I'll tell you another thing. My mum, like, when she got browned off with us she'd say, 'Go and get the cane.' We used to buy a cane round there for a penny, see, and she'd say to my brother – he was the worst – 'Go and get the cane.' 'I'm not going to buy it.' But someone used to go and buy the cane and it was always hanging up and she used to reach up for the cane – only reach up for it, because my dad, being a policeman, he wasn't there a lot.

Memories of mothers often refer to bad temper and physical chastisement – hardly surprising under the circumstances. Gladys Harman, for instance, describes her mother as 'a good mother, but she used to get in a temper. They all did them days.' Fanny Abbott recalls her mother as 'a bit of a tartar'. Yet at the same time, the image of the domineering parent was constantly being undercut by that of the dominated and near-defeated parent.[2] For the children, the behaviour of the parents must have been confusing and ambiguous, and the images they would have begun to shape of adult behaviour equally so. What were they to make of the mother to whom losing sixpence meant so much that the child was frightened to return home, the mother hiding behind the door to evade the landlord, but insisting on honesty from her children? Or the all-powerful father who was suddenly revealed as pitifully vulnerable? Kitty Barnet as a child of twelve could:

> Remember my dad coming home. I'd never seen my dad cry but he burst out crying and my mum was comforting him, saying 'What's the matter, mate?' And he said, he said,

'There was a Tory MP down there' – I even remember his name. His name was Mr Swinnock – and my dad, you know, jumped up and said, 'I want some food for my children. I've got six children at home.' And this chap said to my dad, 'Sit down, pauper.' And he called my dad a pauper, and that cut my dad right to the quick and he really cried.

There were also images of weakness. From her childhood in Vauxhall in the 1920s and 1930s, Sal Beckford recalls her mother too drunk to cope.

. . . times I got my mother home, took her home and made her have a wash. I'd say 'Come on', and I used to give her a bit of lemon so she didn't smell of beer, wash herself, put a clean apron on. I'd say, 'Now look, Mum, when Daddy comes in, don't say anything.' Because it was always her that started the arguments. He'd come in and she'd give him a bloater for his tea. He used to tumble why he'd got a bloater for his tea, because she was out all day long. Anyway, he'd sit having it and he'd say, 'That was very nice. I enjoyed that. Well, what you done today, love?' 'Oh, done a bit of ironing and this, that and the other.' And he'd say 'Well, your nose is red today.' That done it. That started it. 'Your nose is red today, love.' 'Oh, so that's it, is it?' And she'd always done this. 'Well, tomorrow it'll be blue, because I'll be out and I'm telling you now, I'll be out.'

One day he come home. Oh, she was in a state! I found her up the Elephant, standing outside the Rockingham, leaning up against the wall she was. Got her shopping bag there, and I said, 'You do look lovely, where's all your mates now? They've gone and left you.' 'Well, you know who I met? I ain't seen her for years.' That was the excuse. 'Ain't seen her for years.' I said, 'Come on, I'd better get you home out of it.'

We used to have subways then, at the Elephant. There used to be a ladies' toilet there. I took her in there and made her wash her face and hands and all that in there. I said, 'Come on. Twenty to four. Daddy'll be in at four o'clock.'

She'd got this bag. I said, 'What you got in your bag? It was a pease pudding and a faggot, all stuck in a paper bag, all mucked up together. I said, 'What's that for?' I said, 'What you got for Daddy's tea?' 'I thought I'd make him a faggot stew.'

I said, 'You can't make a faggot stew.' There was potato peelings and leaves stuck in there, where she'd been doing the shopping. I had to go and sling it all, didn't I? So I had to run round the corner and get some brawn for me dad's tea. She had no potatoes, so I thought, 'Oh, I don't know what I'm going to do.' Anyway, I remember once when I was doing some shopping for her, we dropped a potato, it rolled underneath the old dresser. I got on the floor and found it. It was a big one which had shoots on it, so I cut all that up, peeled it very fine, cut it and washed it, mashed it all up. That was for my dad's tea, so I wouldn't get her in bleeding trouble.

And images of spite. Rose Parker's father was a butcher.

When I started the job at fourteen I wanted to buy meself a coat in the Cut, course, it was a market then. So my mum said, 'Well, if you save up for it, Rose,' she said, 'I'll help you and we'll get it.' Our mum was the saver.

Well, I was going to have this coat, so she said, 'I'll come down and meet you when you finish.' Well, we worked till gone six at night and I'm telling all the girls at work I'm going to have a new coat, my mum's going to meet me at the corner. When I gets there I sees me mum. So I said, 'Oh, come on, Mum,' I said, 'we might lose the coat.' So she said, 'No, it's still in the window.' And she's crying, so I said, 'What's the matter?' So she said, 'I can't get your coat, Rose.' So I said, 'Why? Why?' So she said, 'The money's gone.' I said, 'The money's gone? Ain't you got it in the front room?' And she said, 'No, it's gone. Your father's had it, I reckon.'

She blew over to my father. He knew what she'd come for. He knew. He sees us coming across the road, and I'm in tears, crying I was. Mum said, 'I want a word with you, Charlie Marshall.' So he said, 'Well, I'm busy.' She said, 'You're not bleeding busy.' She said, 'What have you done with that money? That's the girl's coat money.'

Oh, she wouldn't go home. Wouldn't go home. So all of a sudden his guv'nor come from out the back. He said, 'What's the matter?' He said, 'Oh, don't tell me you took the girl's money.' So my dad said, 'No, I've only borrowed it.' There was a special horse that was going that day and he wanted this money for this horse. That's how he was, my father.

But Violet Harris's father, though he earned insufficient as a labourer at Doulton's for them to afford coal, firewood or a pair of shoes,

> . . . knew all the names of flowers and everything and used to have a beautiful little garden out the back. And when we used to go to Sunday School, we only had a bit of rag for handkerchief, you know. They used to say, 'Bring your handkerchiefs out!' And we had some stuff [in the garden] what they used to call 'old man'. Used to smell like lime. Lovely it was. And he used to say, 'Give them', and he used to press these bits of rag on this old man. Scent, you know.

All the same, Violet commented:

> I can say, really, dear, I never had much of a childhood. And it wasn't no one's fault, really. I was always at their beck and call, lugging them out. We had to go up the park all day long when we had our holidays, so my mother could get on with the washing. She used to say, 'Don't send them home, none of them home, unless you want some tea.' Tea, in a bottle, some bread, all wrapped up in newspaper. And you'd go home and get some more bread and marge, you know? Never got much. Another bottle of tea. Used to be up there about nine o'clock, send us home about six at night.

The eldest girl was always required to shoulder much of the domestic burden, looking after the younger children, running errands, doing housework.

Gracie Tarbuck was born in 1919 and brought up in Vauxhall. She came from a family of seven.

They've [the boys] got it easy. The girls had to do it all. Had to make the beds, sweep the rooms out, scrub the floors, shake the carpet. And if it wasn't done properly you had to turn round and do it all over again. Oh, yes, I've had that. Mother used to come round, 'You haven't done that, girl, get on and do it.'

Many girls resented, if they did not actively resist, the curtailment of their childhood. Nora Chambers was born in Kennington in 1913, the youngest of four children, and the only girl. Her mother died when she was very young, and she was brought up by her father.

I used to say, 'You knock one devil out and two devils in when you chastise me like that.' And I've had a few. But I'm still a rebel, it hasn't knocked the rebel out of me. I used to rebel about the things that you had to do, work, jobs in the house. I couldn't stand it. I couldn't stand doing any housework or anything like that, making my bed. My father said, 'You don't expect your brothers to make your bed.' I said 'I've just cleaned their rooms, why shouldn't they make my bed?'

For the most part, children's lives were lived out in the same space and territory as their mothers': in the street, incorporating play with the everyday world. Childhood was simply part of the continuum of life. Playmates were the same children with whom errands were run; the airey that threatened to swallow the ball, the same airey that swallowed the sixpence. Gracie Tarbuck remembered from her childhood,

> One, two, three, Lairy
> My ball's down the airey
> Don't forget to give it to Mary
> On a Sunday morning

We all had skipping songs. And sevenses, up on the wall. We used to play hopscotch or we used to have the marble, or four or five little stones and play button goal, you'd sit on the kerb and you had to pick them up. And we had dab stones and iron hoops, knock you off the pavement! And we used to play round the lamppost, and knock-down Ginger . . . Mind you, we'd go berserk now, but we used to play knock-down Ginger, didn't we? If you get kids keep knocking at your door and running away, you'd go berserk, in't you? But we all done it, especially in the buildings, tie a bit of string on the bottom one and loop it all the way through . . .

Queenie Thomas described how:

We used to have one of those great big thick ropes, and you used to be right across the street playing skipping, you know, and you really enjoyed that. And then, you know, the old street lamps, we used to throw our rope over that bar and have a swing round till the lamp lighter came along. We'd say, 'Quick, here he comes', and we used to pull our rope off and run . . .

(My mother recalled Good Friday skipping with ship's hawsers – with competitions between adults and children – and such skipping chants as:

> There's somebody under the bed
> I don't know who it is
> It makes me feel so frightened
> So N . . . come in and see.[3])

Marjorie Rowlands and Viley Neal were sisters, born in 1925 and 1926 respectively. They were born and brought up in the Elephant and Castle, and still share the same house to which they moved just after the war.

We used to have to take the sandwiches to my father, fresh, every day. Come out of school . . . Mondays, we used to have to come home and wash, well, rinse, blue and starch all the washing, put it through the wringer. Then it would be a fight

as to who was going to take the sandwiches, to get out of
doing the washing ... every Thursday night, had to help
mother to do the housework ...

All physical space was already occupied by adults. The
child's world therefore was closely observed and any attempt
by the children to create some private space often brought
them into conflict with adults. Marjorie Rowlands and Viley
Neal talked of 'The old-fashioned policeman, used to move
you off the street corners with a flip with his glove, you know,
"On your way".' Most adults were able to command and
control children, whether their own or those of a neighbour.
Brushes with grown-ups were part of the normal pattern and
mirrored brushes between adults and authority.

At the same time, the fact that time and space were policed
by neighbours and relatives meant that children could be
allowed the freedom to roam. Marjorie and Viley also talked of
this.

Many's the time we spent down the old subway [at the
Elephant and Castle]. Not this subway, the old one that used
to be. I mean, this is a monster compared to the other one.
But we used to go down there on skates, get your ears
clipped, you know, for going down on skates.

There used to be a courtway in our street, used to lead
right down into St George's Road again. It was the courtway
to a picture palace, this courtway, and we used to come out
this courtway and go three or four doors along, and this was
our house. Well, we used to go up there on a Saturday
morning, me and my brother, to the pictures, the tuppenny
gaff as they called it, the old piano 'da di da di la'. See all the
shows, like 'Love on the Dole', 'Sweeney Todd', and
varieties and that, all those sort of things. And then all of a
sudden the back door would open: 'Margie! Viley!' Your
dinner's ready!' And we used to have to come out, Most of
them used to come out as well because 'If their dinner's
ready, so is ours!'

Just as the child's world was an integral part of the adult world, the space the same space, the roles the same roles, so, too, the deceptions were the same. The nursery permitted fantasy, but for these children the gap which they perceived between appearance and reality – the world of make-believe – was not a luxury of their making, but ever present in the fabric of life.

This gap between appearance and reality, between hope and fact, was brought sharply, and sometimes cruelly, into focus at Christmas time. Queenie Thomas:

> We were upstairs and we had our stockings hanging on the bed. We didn't get Christmas stockings then, we put our own black stockings. And then when we woke up I said, 'Look at my stocking! Isn't it filled up?' Well, of course, when we opened it my father went and put Brussels sprouts, potatoes, everything in the stocking. So, what we done, we knew he was going out so we lifted the bedroom window – we slept in the front – so as he was walking down the street, all of a sudden he got pelted with potatoes and Brussels sprouts. Supposed to have been for our Christmas dinner . . .

Sal Beckford:

> One Christmas I woke. I hung me stocking up and when I wakes up I looks to see if Father Christmas had been. The stocking was hanging up, there was an orange at the bottom of it and I thought, 'Oh, it's all full up.' There was all the things off the chest of drawers in my stocking for me presents. All of them. I thought 'Oh, Father Christmas has been good to me' and I gets all the ornaments . . . my brother said, 'Don't cry.'

Violet Harris, however, remembers how:

> Mum used to try and make it as nice a Christmas as she could and that was the only time, like once a year, that we got a bit of lump sugar in our tea. And that was the only time the

pictures got a birthday, because they was all taken down and cleaned and put up again.

We only got a rig-out once a year. That was Christmas. She used to go in a little club down the Walk. You put some money on a card and you could draw it out, like, Christmas. And she scraped, bless her heart. Every farthing she'd put away. And she'd make us, my Lily, my Beattie and me, she'd be ages in her spare time at night, making these petticoats and these nick-drawers like. Well, by the time we cast them off at Christmas, they was in rags, wasn't they? We never got no more. We never got no more clothes. Never had a coat. Never knew what a coat was. Or hat. No, no. That was our lot.

But the gap between appearances and reality, the deception, was relentless and year-long. It was part of the culture, of the armoury of survival, part of the rhythm and structure of life. Deception became reality, at the same time as it was a symbol of how life should be lived.

Outward appearances were always important. Kate East recalled her mother.

Mother had always foraged . . . she always tried to get meals and always kept a regular time for meals and if they hadn't got anything for dinner and you'd got to cut up bread and jam, she always put the cloth on for dinner time, see. There was the regular time.

Tricia Dempsey was born in Vauxhall in 1935. Before the war, her father worked mainly as a delivery man.

My dad was very, very critical, that you kept your shoes cleaned. He'd polish and show us how to polish our shoes and there'd be holes underneath with cardboard in, but the tops would shine and we used to be proud of our shoes, you know? Sometimes we'd be picked out, 'Who's got the cleanest shoes?' in school, and you know we'd think, ooh, we're somebody because our shoes were all sparkling. But underneath, we got cardboard.

Keeping up appearances was a point of pride and a rallying call for the family's morale. Reality may have been displaced, but the belief in appearances and their importance – the grown-up world of make-believe – was often all that could be said to be private and personal. Deception became a form of resistance, a form of protection for the family when intrusions from outside could all too easily disrupt the equilibrium. Queenie Thomas recalled the time when:

> They sent me to the cleansing station, and, honestly, it was terrible. They said I'd got nits. My mum said, 'You ain't got nits. You've got scurf.' Well, I had to go. And they washed your hair with paraffin, and they get a nit comb and they combed it through with sassafras. Well, you stunk when you come out. And it wasn't. It wasn't nits.
>
> Ever since then my mum used to say to me 'Come on here.' Soft soap she used to get from Douglas (the chemist) and she used to do these chips in the oven, quassia chips and you used to put that on your hair and comb it through. And she used to have to buy these tiny fine steel combs, they used to call them nit combs. She used to get this great big sheet of newspaper, like that, all over and wait for them to drop out. But nothing ever dropped out.

With the world of make-believe a deadly serious game, played by adults, what space was there for childhood fantasy and imaginings? Childhood was haunted by a world of real-life ogres. Sal Beckford remembers when:

> The school board man was coming round. 'Why ain't you at school?' I said, 'I'm waiting to see the insurance man.' So he said 'The insurance man? Your mother's never paid insurance money.' I said, 'Well, that's what she said. I've got to see the insurance man.'

And Nora Chambers remembers:

> There was Miss Dangerfield, she was my teacher, at St Saviour's Salamanca. She was a bitch. She caned me once

for something. For talking. I was turning and talking to a girl behind me and I was caught. She had me out in front of the class and she said, 'I'm going to give you three strokes.' So I said, 'Well, that's a lot.' She said, 'Don't talk to me. Hold your hand out.' She gave me three and she marked me across me hand and she hurt me, and I never cried. So she said, 'Put your hand out again, I evidently haven't hurt you enough.' So I said, 'You have hurt me.' I said, 'Look.' She said, 'Show them me', the stripes on me hand, and she gave me another one and, oh, I cried then, because she did hurt me.

School was a major intervention into the child's life. Many children disliked school, and many parents regarded it with ambivalence. While the school safely controlled the child for the major part of the day, it was also through the school that other agents were able to intervene – sometimes benevolently, in the provision of breakfast, milk and a midday meal, but often malevolently, in the form of the school nurse (or 'Nitty Nora'), or the school board man. For the nurse or the school attendance officer brought an authority which extended out of the school and directly into the home. It was part of the armada of state intervention which always loomed on the horizon.

As far as Queenie Thomas was concerned, school was a waste of time.

They learnt you to do like a little bit of laundry and we used to be all morning, say, washing six handkerchiefs and ironing them. They used to call it hygiene. We used to do like one year housework, then the second year was cookery and then the third year like laundry. Learnt to make the bed and bath the baby. Pretty useless because as I say you used to spend all the morning doing something that was very trifling. Learn you how to sweep the chimney, how to shop and all that sort of thing.

Education for girls was often seen as expendable. Violet Harris remembers:

My mum said to me 'Stay away today, Violet, I got that washing to finish.' I said, 'Don't want to.' 'You've got to look after him' – one of the kids. It hadn't got much after two o'clock before someone come over for me – I lived right near the school, see. 'Oh, Mrs Fowler, Violet coming to school?' 'No,' she says, 'she's not well.' I was all right, mind.

Most girls left school at fourteen and went straight to work. Marjorie Rowlands and Viley Neal:

I wouldn't say there was enough interest to have made us want to stay at school. Really and truly, and being a girl as well, you were never pushed as girls, least I don't think so. Not in our time. You were just expected to get married and have a family and that was it. You left and went to work, and that was it.

Rene Grant:

I passed the scholarship. Then someone told my mother that you had to buy all the pens and pencils and she said, 'I've kept you for fourteen years,' she said, 'you'll have to keep yourself now.'

When the Second World War broke out in 1939, Lambeth was particularly vulnerable to bombing, and many children born just before or during the war spent their childhood as evacuees, or in the centre of the blitz.

Judy Chalmers, the daughter of a dockworker, lived at the Elephant and Castle:

1937 I was born. We was bombed out of Holyoak Road and we were put into a rest centre and my mother was expecting a baby, so I was evacuated and my sister was evacuated.

The first people that I went to was a very old religious couple that kept wanting to take me to chapel and watching the husband play bowls on a Sunday evening. I didn't like them very much at all. Then they moved me to another woman who'd got a little boy and I think I was too much of a problem for her. She took me back to the Rehabilitation Centre – I think she only had me a fortnight. She didn't like me. I suppose being taken away from my parents I turned into a wet-bed case and I can remember coming home from school and she'd got the neighbours in, showing them the wet sheets, what she'd got to put up with.

And then I went to another family who I think was solely doing it for the eight bob [40p] a week, because they had loads of us and they were all right, they didn't ill-treat us or anything like that, but I mean, there was no particular fondness, they were there for the eight bob.

I suppose the London children were that little bit rougher. We all went from the street, you was all with your friends and you didn't particularly miss your parents. I think I used to sort of play-act that I did. My mother came up to see me a couple of times. Then every couple of weeks she'd send a parcel, a food parcel, and she used to make sweets out of shredded wheat and that sort of thing. In fact, the people that we stayed with thought that they was millionaires compared to them up there. When my father and mother came down and took them out for a drink, they thought he was a millionaire because he'd got a pound note in his pocket.

There was a five-year age gap between me and my sister so I suppose, after the war when we all came back, I resented her because you do don't you at that age? And then when I'd come back and I'd got this angel of a little brother who couldn't do no wrong . . . I don't think I was particularly pleased to be back.

For many children, like Tricia Dempsey, war was part of normality.

I can't ever remember being frightened and we were in Vauxhall all through the war. Areas had been flattened in Vauxhall Street. I remember the shelters and all down on the floor and it was all a big game. I can't ever remember being scared. And I used to think, 'Oh, there's an air-raid warning, oh, leave me here, what did you wake me up for?'

'Come on, you've got to come down the shelter.' Hated it, going down the shelter. The underground. The smell. That damp, disinfectant smell of the toilets. But when we went down the Oval, I mean, me nan and me great-grandad used to go and they always used to have the same two bunks on the corner, just as you came down the moving stairs. You kind of booked them and you left things there, rolled up blanket and a pillow, and you'd leave it there. No one would think of pinching it.

For children the post-war environment of damaged or blitzed terraces and buildings represented a landscape of adventure, rather than dereliction. As Tricia recalled again:

We played in the bombed-out ruins of Doulton's, I could always be found there. I enjoyed myself one afternoon climbing up the chimney from the inside and looking out over London. Mum would have had a fit! We'd take dolls and toys and play in the empty rooms high up. Most of the floors only had the beams to walk on. But then children could go off anywhere to play. We roamed the area all the time.

Teresa Malloy was born in 1956, the child of Irish immigrants who, having failed to make a way in the United States, came to England and settled around Kennington and the Elephant and Castle. As a child, Teresa thought: 'bomb sites were all right. Well, at least it was somewhere to play . . .'

The pre-war constants of poverty and poor housing were perceptibly changing. This change was itself the constant for the post-war child, to whom the bomb sites offered a place to play, through which to live out the imaginings of childhood. Beyond the papered chimney stacks, the doors opening into emptiness, the exposed cellars, their future world was being built.

After the war, Tricia Dempsey's father secured a job with the electricity board. Her mother worked the twilight shifts as a cleaner. Tricia's early years were spent in buildings with a shared toilet and no bathroom, but, benefiting by the post-war development, her family secured a modern council flat.

After the war we moved into a posh new block of council flats, Dolland House, in Vauxhall Street. First time we'd ever seen a bath! And an Ascot! And I had a bedroom for the first time. Life was just great! They were kept spotlessly clean and the kids – no kids were allowed out late, walking, making a noise on the stairs or in the grounds. Everyone belonged together, a gang in each block, playing and skipping. Most Sundays a gang of us would be taken by one of the dads in the block swimming, to Kennington Baths. If you got there before eight o'clock it was free.

For the parents, life was still far from easy.

When you think, it must have been hard, you didn't realise as kids, but it must have been hard, immediately after the war. In the pawn shop, everybody did it. They managed and scratched through. I think back to what we had when we were young, and you had bare boards scrubbed and wooden tables scrubbed and newspaper on the table for Sunday and you always had winkles and shrimps because they were very cheap for Sunday tea and you only had afters once a week and it was Sunday and it was always custard and jelly. I remember the first time I ever tasted a jelly after the war. Mum had told us about jelly. And we had green jelly! Often you'd come home from school and your main meal of the day was the school dinner and tea would be your bread dipped in sugar or you might be lucky and you'd say, 'Oh, butter tonight, Mum.' 'Yes, only a quarter.' You know, still on rations.

We never had a holiday. No one had a car. One year, in September time, we were asked if we would like to share a bin with a family who were going hop picking. This must have been 1948, '49. Mum packed the old pram with blankets and jumpers and pots and pans. But we all went with half a dozen other families, all packed into a lorry and driven to Kent for three or four weeks.

Bushels of hops were measured by the basket. Eight old pence [3p] a bushel. Three or four in a family would pick all day from about half past seven to five, and manage about thirty to thirty-five bushels. It was hard on your hands and the binds would be sharp and your fingers would be black from the hops. And Dad would tempt us with ideas of bikes and scooters for Christmas if we picked. But we'd feign bellyaches and toothaches and any pain that would keep us off the field and get us down to the Medway river or scrumping or get the faggots for burning on the fire.

All the same, for Tricia's family the weekly budget was becoming less tight: 'Although my dad never earned a lot of money, he always had a pound in his pocket, always had a pound in his pocket.' And the family moved in step with the growing affluence of the 1950s.

But there was a different, equally typical, experience of growing up in the post-war environment. Although Lambeth's housing programme continued apace there were still many unable to take advantage of it. Industry in the area was declining, and skilled jobs were becoming increasingly difficult to get locally. The affluence of the 1950s and 1960s passed some families by, and the life patterns and chances of many people appeared little different from those of their parents.

Teresa Malloy's family moved from one substandard property to another, until their social worker finally found them secure council accommodation. The family lived in fear of being split up, of the children being taken into care because of the parents' apparent inability to cope.

Because somehow, when you're poor and because you're Irish, and because you've got a lot of kids and because you live in a slum, they felt that if they let us go, they'd never see us again.

Most of my childhood has been very, very poor. Very basic. Very much cardigans ripped and knitted for the other kids, and all the school jumpers were always hand-made. All your clothes were hand-made but it looked it, and we didn't like that. Me mum would never go to jumble sales. And if me dad was out of work we had a small bit of meat on the Sunday – but the rest of the time you sort of had eggs and stuff, scrambled eggs a lot, and beans on toast a lot . . .

The disparity between relative affluence and poverty was not new. But the atmosphere in which this disparity now appeared was. Clearly, the inauguration of the Welfare State, the post-war housing renewal policy, the political slogans of the governing Tory party under Macmillan asserted that there was affluence: yet by the mid-1960s, for instance, the Child Poverty Action Group had been formed with the aim of exposing the gaps in provision and opportunity and eradicating poverty.

There had been a subtle twist to the timeless division between the 'haves' and 'have nots', for the 'have nots' now, in theory, should not exist.

Between the wars, poverty was perceived as being structural, and the strategies for survival, both material and imaginary, were rooted in the social structure. But in the post-war period, poverty began to be perceived (again) as personal, and, as affluence became the norm, poverty began to assume an aura of immorality. 'We was all in the same boat', a strong collective feeling, no longer applied.

The child's world and the adult's world were no longer so closely synchronised. The values, life-styles and expectations of an older generation appeared inappropriate and inapplicable to the children of the Welfare State. Moreover, childhood began to offer space in which a different definition could be created. The absolute authority of adults no longer seemed to apply. Many memories of post-war childhood describe rebellion.

Tricia Dempsey:

I always hopped the wag. You could do it easily in that school. You could go in and get your mark and there was so many different classrooms, you'd have to leave your teacher then and go to one of these teachers. I'd just come out then and then go back for lunch time to be marked in in the afternoon. You could do that all the time and I often did that.

Teresa Malloy:

A lot of the school rules seemed so stupid that I actually couldn't fit in with them. I was never expelled or suspended or anything like that, it was always borderline – is she or is she not being really impertinent, is she trying to really wind me up? Or go in East Lane and skive out, and that was really good. Got caught. Always got caught, always. I just always looked like I was about to cause trouble. I think I've got one of those faces! And fights. I used to fight with anyone, didn't matter, boy or girl. I used to fight if I thought they were in the wrong. And football. I used to love football. I used to be good at football as well. But you start to get to an age and everyone's saying 'Oh you must wear a dress and don't do that, Teresa.'

Occasionally, resistance was overtly against a parent. Maggie Thorpe was born in 1957, on an interwar estate in Vauxhall, where she still lives.

I was a terror! When we lived down with me nan, me dad was away and I had long hair. It was really long. And I would not come in and over the road we used to go to shops and I wouldn't come in and me mum chased me, and I made her chase me all the way round and then me other sister come in, she's waiting on the corner and I've not seen her and she dragged me – oh, it didn't half hurt – dragged me hair, all along the ground.

Karen West, a friend of Maggie's, was born in Vauxhall in 1962 and now lives on the same estate with her two children. As a child, she remembers:

I was a little tearaway. Staying out till eleven o'clock at night. From the age of eight to sixteen I was away, because I . . .

wouldn't settle down in school. But when I was home on me holidays I was out, climbing on the sheds, knocking on the doors, staying out late when I should have come in and that.

But most of those tearaways of the 1950s and 1960s now lead, in the 1970s and 1980s, lives that appear as restricted and as class-bound as those of their mothers.

For many, the hope that was once theirs is now focused on the babies. Karen Howard is now a single parent of two young children, and lives with her widowed mother in a council flat in Kennington, but:

> I want Mark to go to a nice school, some discipline, you know what I mean? Because we was spoilt and we was easygoing. But I'd like it different for him. I'd like him to be something. I'd like him to go to university. I've all these things builded up in me head, things I want them to do. He wants to be a fire engine man, of all things, put out the fires. No, he can't be that. I said to him one time, I'm putting you in the Navy. Oh, I'd love that I would, really would.

Jackie Davy was born in 1958 and came to live in Kennington when she married her husband, a printer with the (former) Greater London Council. They live in a flat owned by the Duchy of Cornwall, where her husband's parents also live.

> We're not snobs, but we're certainly not like some people. We don't want them [the children] to mix . . . perhaps we are snobs . . . we don't want them to mix with too many people in this block of flats, for instance. The neighbours laugh at us – 'You're always watching them', this, that and the other. But it makes no difference to us. They can laugh all they like. My friends have a dig at me and say, you know, 'What's wrong with letting them down there [into the square], it's good enough for my children, why isn't it good enough for yours?' Well, it's not good enough for my children. They come first, and getting out of here is part of it. We've got to get out of here. That's why I do childminding, that's why I work Saturdays, and Pete does overtime. We just can't imagine

letting them loose on the street. There's nowhere nice for them to go. And there's no decent school round here and I believe in education. I think they're bright and I just want them to use that brightness without having disruption. We know what goes on in the classrooms and there's no way you can learn . . .

References

1.   Maud Pember Reeves, *Round About a Pound a Week*.
2.   See Carolyn Steedman, *Landscape for a Good Woman*, Virago, London, 1986.
3.   My father recalled singing:

> There was a Scotch Heelander
> He went to Waterloo
> The wind blew up his petticoats
> And showed his cockadoodledoo . . .

and

> At the cross, at the cross
> Where the Kaiser lost his horse
> And the eagle on his flat flew away
> He was eating German buns
> When he heard the British guns
> And now he's running, running, running all away.

CHAPTER 4

Stepping Out

It is obvious that with [both these] young men marriage is, so far, both pleasant and successful . . . The young women's lives are far more changed. They tell you that, though they are a bit lonely at times, and miss the companionship of the factory life and the money of their own to spend, and are rather frightened at the swift approach of motherhood, you get accustomed to it . . .[1]

Leaving school and starting work is always an important step: the end of childhood and the entry into adulthood. For many working-class girls in the period between the wars (as now) there was no luxury of adolescence, no space and time for adjustment between childhood and adulthood. Few working-class families could afford the money or time for education (other than training on the job), or, even, for contemplation to come to terms with self, family, class and adulthood.

For a girl caught in the paradoxes of growing up, in the transition from child and dependent to the new status of wage-earner, starting work could be a bewildering time.

The need to work and the imperatives of working were a central part of the culture. Girls, of course, had always worked in the home. It was part of their domestic schooling. Going out to work, for girls, was seen as an extension of their existing contribution, a contribution now paid in cash rather than in services or kind. Girls were expected to hand over their wages to their mothers.

When Molly Nelson started work, about 1915:

I used to take the half-crown [12½p] home on a Friday night. She used to give me tuppence [1p]. That's for working all the week.

The experience of Violet Harris was similar:

I used to start out eight o'clock in the morning to get there by nine. I was at work till seven o'clock at night and I used to get home at eight. For 2s.6d. [12½p] a week. Saturday and all. Nine till two, Saturday. Don't even remember having a dinner hour. Young kid, you know, and when I got home I give mother the half a crown. She used to give me thruppence [1½p] back.

This contribution was partly to pay for their keep, but also partly a return payment for their upbringing, as Queenie Thomas put it.

I done an apprenticeship in dressmaking, in Hanover Square. I had to do five years' apprenticeship and when I started work it was 6s. [30p] a week. When I finished, I was getting 9s. [95p]. And then I moved. I had to leave that job because you couldn't get good money in the same job, and the next job I got was 35s. [£1.75], and I was nineteen then. And then I went and got married . . . Yeah, my mum never benefited at all from me.

With few girls allowed to keep more than pocket money from their earnings, working was no guarantee of independence. But work offered companionship, solidarity and, often, fun.
Carrie Telford's mother

. . . wanted me to get out of the factory. She said, 'I don't like that place.' It was, like, a bottle factory. They all used to swear a lot but believe me, those girls were the nicest girls anyone could have spoken to. Although they swore, if you were a friend of theirs, you were a friend, and don't matter what you did or anybody come up to you, they'd be by your side all the time. Nobody could touch you, not if you had those as friends. Marvellous girls. But they just took swear words in their stride, you know?

Starting work clearly involved a shift in status. But it also involved a shift in culture and, occasionally, class.

Violet Harris began work as a tailor's runner.

Do you know, I was really in the land of enchantment there. These beautiful women. It would take you right to fairyland. They had lovely hair and these lovely, beautiful, glistening gowns. It really took me, you know, in a daze. Even used to have their knickers tailored. Can you imagine?

While I was there, one of the girls rigged me up. Took me out, bought me some bloomers because she said the Jew boy used to look up me clothes because I had no drawers on. Bought me some bloomers . . .

But even more important to the girls than their transfer to the world of work was their developing sexuality. There was a physical and psychological maturing as puny and undeveloped fourteen-year-olds became, within four years or so, mothers themselves. It was a process where there was some potential for conflict between themselves and their parents. Many parents imposed constraints on their daughters which were at variance not only with those imposed on their brothers, but with the girls' own experience as children. Girls were simply not as free to come and go, especially at night.

Gracie Tarbuck recalls how:

I had to be in at ten. My dad would be waiting for me on the doorstep. He chased me all round our street one night because I was late. And I had to stop in all the bloody week. Sent to bed. 'I'll give you boys!' he said. I used to lose all my boyfriends.

So long as a girl stayed under her parents' roof, she was expected to conform to the authority and needs of her parents. And yet, leaving home and living independently as a single woman was not an option. Some lived with aunts or other relatives or took a room in a neighbour's house, but this was largely to alleviate the problems of overcrowding rather than an assertion of independence. Some girls left home temporarily to go into service. But for the most part girls lived at home, which was considered both proper and appropriate. Yet against such propriety, a new standard was emerging.

Throughout the 1920s and 1930s there was a steady expansion of office and shop work in London, and an increasing number of girls came to London from the provinces in search of work. Some employers, like the Oxford Street department store Bourne and Hollingsworth, offered their own protected accommodation for their employees, but many girls had to find lodgings of their own. And a young single girl living by herself, or with a friend, was open to the suspicion of being 'fast'. The ambiguity surrounding the new independent worker could be found in the fine-tuning of such popular weeklies as *Titbits*, where, for example, one editorial, in that unique mix of the prurient and the cautionary, warned of the dangers of loneliness for young girls living by themselves, and the easy prey they represented for men prepared to befriend for more sinister motives.[2]

But while a shop girl's or a stenographer's wages may have been sufficient to allow her to live independently, the local Lambeth girl starting work as a factory worker or apprentice simply did not earn enough to pay for rent as well as food and clothing. (Few seemed to become stenographers and those who entered shop work did so in local rather than West End shops.) Moreover, since many were married by their late teens, or early twenties, the period in which they might have been independent was short: so the respectable London girl remained, for practical as well as moral reasons, at home.

For most of these girls the only viable and acceptable alternative to home was marriage. There was considerable social pressure from family and friends to 'settle down', a pressure that was reinforced in films and women's magazines, which extolled the virtues of home and marriage, and offered a new ideal of wife and mother. *Woman's Own* was launched in 1932 as the 'new weekly for the modern young wife who loves her home ... any girl worth her salt wants to be the best housewife ever – and then some'.[3]

Marriage was seen as a natural progression to the next and inevitable stage in life, courtship the means to that end. Parental resistance to boy-friends did not mean that they were opposed to courtship in itself, but it did represent an anxiety: for on the one hand marriage would mean the loss of their daughter's help and earnings; on the other, courtship was a demonstration of sexuality, of independence, that could lead as easily to the path of ruin as to marriage.

Lily White recalls how:

My father used to be on the doorstep at ten o'clock if I wasn't in. He used to say, 'What you can't do on the inside, don't do on the entry.' There was no – not like there is today. You'd get put away, wouldn't you?

Molly Nelson said:

We didn't know nothing when we was sixteen or eighteen. We didn't know nothing about sex, and that's the truth. Didn't know nothing about this bloody sex business. My poor mother would turn me out if I went with a boy-friend. She'd take me by the hair 'Come 'ere!' You couldn't have your legs showing years ago. My poor mother would say, 'Good Gawd Almighty, put your clothes down.' My mother used to say of those girls, 'Dirt. They're trollops. They're no good.'

If daughters were constrained by the potential wrath of their parents, they were also constrained by ignorance. Moral guidance was offered in a vacuum of ignorance and misinformation. Many parents, mothers particularly, were themselves too embarrassed to talk of sex, or lacked an easy vocabulary with which to express it. What guidance they could offer was couched in terms of the visible experience and symbols of their culture: tarts and trollops and the rest.

But for the interwar generation this was clearly becoming insufficient. The symbols themselves were changing and losing their meaning. The iconography of womanhood was transformed during this period. The role models of mature women, as represented by mothers and older female relatives, were increasingly supplemented, and contradicted, and replaced, by images of women transmitted through the media of films and magazines. Such images offered a pleasure which indulged both the imagination and the senses, which presented a future and an escape. And these externally manufactured images of women inevitably altered the attitudes young women had to themselves.

Make-up, for instance, was becoming acceptable. Make-up was fantasy realised, the means to transformation. And it was attainable. Even if the products of the large international cosmetic houses were way beyond the reach of the working-class pocket, there were cheaper imitations. In Woolworth's, small Rimmel powders, lipsticks and rouge sold for 3*d*. (1½p) or 6*d*. (2½p), and Phul-nana powders and lipsticks for as little as 2*d*. (1p).

Young Lambeth girls still had very little money to spare for clothes; but now it was enough to enable them to dress fashionably. The factory girl's clothes still differed from the rich girl's in the quality of the fabric and in finish, but the style was quite likely to be similar. Fashionable styles had become simpler, and therefore easier to mass-produce, and increasingly accessible to the working girl. They could be bought 'off the peg', by mail order and by instalments. 'Modish frocks', such as a 'Corot model', with contemporary and significant names like 'the Stenographer' were advertised at 3 guineas (£3.15), or 9*s*. (45p) a month. They could be bought even more cheaply in the market, in Lambeth Walk or East Lane, where dresses sold for much less than one pound. And, if they could not be bought, they could be made. Good-quality fabric was sold in the market at 3*s*. 11*d*. (19p) a yard. Books of patterns, like *Weldon's Home Dressmaker*, cost 4*d*. (2p); *Titbits* offered special bargain patterns which could be bought for 4½*d*.

Ordinary patterns only cost 6*d*. (2½p). Mass-produced dress-making patterns had the advantage of being able to be used again and lent around, and, providing there was access to a sewing machine, the end-product was likely to be of far superior quality to any manufactured garment, for half the price. A new frock could be made for under 12*s*. (60p). Zip fasteners and press studs had made skilled buttonholing unnecessary.

With little money but some ingenuity, the factory girl could transform herself, if only for an evening, into a 'somebody', wearing a frock from the Walk, Bemberg stockings at 2*s*.11*d*. (14p) a pair, or Woolworth's stockings at 6*d*. (2½p) each, carrying in her handbag five Weights at 2*d*. (1p), or, daringly, some Abdullah cigarettes, along with a Phul-nana scent card, 1*d*. (½p) a go from machines around the Elephant, and dabbing behind her ears a little Californian Poppy or Ashes of Roses, or some Soir de Paris by Bourgeois.

Ada Terry describes going out around 1933, when she was sixteen.

> My mother had a fur coat, as she got on better, you know, a black fur coat, and she didn't want it so me and my friend, we cut it up and made a shoulder fur, and we had big hats. We didn't have nothing else to wear, you know, to make ourselves look nice, to get a chap. Went to the cinema. We weren't half going to have a good time . . .

Such fashion might have been at variance with a deeper, lived reality, with the overcrowding of home, the tensions of slum life and the possible resentments of parents for whom such luxuries, such frivolities, mocked and diminished their own youths. But it was also part of the new reality for young women in the 1920s and 1930s. Dressing fashionably and 'smartly', dressing according to taste, in new clothes, was one way in which to define an independence and a difference from their childhood and from their mothers, for whom clothing was often, perforce, of secondary importance. The shabbiness of their mothers, never seen with 'a nice costume, a nice coat' but always in 'what she used to call her everyday coat. Old black thing, all shining . . .' (Violet Harris) was now often perceived for the first time. And the difference between the child who had known no coat, no wardrobe ('we didn't have no wardrobe'), and the adult who could afford to buy a 'smart little outfit' – even though only one or two years would have separated the two – was significant. 'Clothes used to be handed down,' said Queenie Thomas, 'and I had five older sisters, so you can imagine. Before I went to work and earned some money, I hardly ever had anything new . . .'

And even though the 'smart little outfit' may have been the only little outfit, it, and the woman beneath, stood, if only temporarily, for something else. However large the gap between appearance and reality, a duality with which many were familiar by this time, young women were at the centre of the illusion, its creators. To look glamorous was to feel important, for all around such glamour promised success. The new office worker, or the shop girl in the quality store, looked smart; short stories in magazines placed appearance in lieu of the fairy godmother as poor girls dressed their way to fortune and happiness. Nora Chambers:

> I've always kept meself as regards me top clothes, I've always scraped enough to get, to look decent. I know I went for a job at, sold books, in Victoria Street and I wanted a job badly. And I saw the advert in the paper and I went and I got it. I was there quite a long time. And he [the boss] was talking one day, like, about me working, he said, 'Your work is very satisfactory. I took you on your appearance.' He said, 'I thought you were a customer when you came through the door. You did look nice.' And I had a grey tailored costume.

Asked if she'd made her own clothes,

> No. I couldn't make anything. I couldn't cut out for one thing. But I like shop things, really. Well, then I've always found somebody that's had them to sell, you know, cheap . . . [or] you used to order them from a book, you see, and pay so much a week. That was how I always kept myself looking decent.

Looking decent, looking smart, was the visual elevator out of class. Health and youth were commodities to be prized. 'Be tall', commanded the small ads in *Titbits*, 'with the Stebbing system. Height increased 3–5 inches. Complete course 5*s*. [25p].' Long, slender lines were the symbol of the new girl: 'Simplicity on long lines,' intoned *Weldon's Home Dressmaker*. Ovaltine promised the 'grace and charm that spring from radiant health'. While the photographic images of women athletes portrayed muscularity as health, the line drawings of the fashion advertisements and of magazine illustrations offered images of leggy, slender women. Advice was given on slimming, on diet and exercise. All appeared part of a national celebration of health, of the triumph over the short and weedy physiques that had characterised the working class of Edwardian Britain. In the 1930s height/weight charts, such as those published by the London County Council, emphasised the taller Briton – even though at this time unemployment was the worst in the twentieth century.

For young working-class women, fashion had never been available in such abundance. Elegance was no longer something to be admired and envied in the affluent: it was within reach of the ordinary working girl. Skinny little kids could adorn fashion and gaze at themselves in the pages of the new women's magazines (as well as *Woman's Own* there was *Woman*, which began in 1937) or the popular daily press.

But there was so little time before the child became the mother: dressing up and courtship appeared to merge into a single function, and that function elided into the certain prospect of marriage. The dangers of domesticity to the new woman were not totally overlooked – even though the fact that 'married women lose their looks' was simply ascribed to their neglecting to take Wincarnis tonic.[4]

Early adulthood meant courtship.

Emmie Dunstan was born in 1919, and brought up in Lambeth Walk.

Lambeth Baths used to hold dances, and that's where we met. But I had to be back at ten o'clock. I've seen my father coming to meet me, to see that I come out. Mind you, my husband was the same, you know, even the boys didn't stop out like they do now, none of that business with them.

Queenie Thomas recalls how:

. . . as you got older, you got a young man to take you. Well, if he took you in the one-and-nines [8p], the one-and-nines in the front of the circle, oh, you was millionaires, you know? A sixpenny [2½p] ice cream . . .

Sue Dexter was born in Lancashire in 1915 and came down to London into domestic service:

I met Fred when I was working in service as a lady's maid and he used to deliver caviare and all the luxury foods from where he was working. We got chatting, as young people do anyway, and he asked me to go out with him and I was sort of over the moon because somebody had asked me out. I had no friends in London until then, really. So I met him and we started going out regularly on my days off.

I was seventeen. I would meet him out, come over here from where I was working in Belgravia and get on the tram and meet him outside the Blue Café in Westminster Bridge Road. We'd go in there and we'd have egg and chips and bread and butter and tea, all for sixpence [2½p]. Sit there practically all day and then go for a stroll.

But eldest daughters, whether working or courting, were still required to mind the younger children, and help out in the house, so what time there might be for courting was heavily constrained by domestic obligations.

Ada Terry:

We always had to mind them [the children], always had to look after them. Even when I was courting, I used to have to go out on the block doorway to have a little kiss, and then have to run back to see if the kids were all right, honest. I done my courting in our block doorways down there, and then go back and see if the kids was all right.

Marjorie Rowlands and Viley Neal recalled how:

Thursdays we used to have to stay in and do the housework. Well, my job was the stairs, all the stairs in the house and the passage. And I guarantee every Thursday, a knock at the door, and he'd be standing there. 'I'm not coming round any more. I'd rather go out with me mates . . .'

Nevertheless, however much it may have been resisted or resented by both parents, courtship was a legitimate activity for young girls to engage it. Few working-class girls failed to get married. But at the same time, opportunities for meeting boys were confined to and by the neighbourhood. Indeed, the street was where many couples met and carried on their courtship.[5] Marriage was often to the first boy who showed an interest. The fear of being 'left on the shelf' was given an added urgency by the shelf in question – an overcrowded, restrictive and exploitative home which was sharply at variance with the new woman.

Courtship often began early. Marjorie Rowlands is not untypical.

I went with my husband when I was fourteen. Broke off when I was about fifteen. Went back together again. I think I was really going out with him serious about fifteen and got engaged when I was sixteen . . .

In the 1930s marriage at eighteen was not at all unusual, and few people considered eighteen too young to marry. But however mature an eighteen-year-old girl may have appeared, having had four years out at work and, undoubtedly, considerable domestic experience, there was often an innocence which created an emotional myopia, an enthusiasm which got the better of her judgement.

Many parents were genuinely concerned about their daughter's choice of husband: they were only too well aware that marrying the 'wrong' man could mean a life of misery and hardship. And with the realism of experience, their view of whether a man was 'wrong' or 'right' was determined by whether he had a regular job as much as by temperament.

Amy Green was born in 1913 and at eighteen married a coster in Lambeth Walk. Although they found accommodation in a Guinness flat,

> My mum used to think it was terrible, because my dad had a regular job, and he went mad when he seen me struggling. I think it was what finished him off because he saw me having an awful life and that, and he never said much but he didn't have to be told anything, my dad. You see, my dad used to sort of feel for you, care about you . . .

In some cases pregnancy forced the marriage and, even in memories told some fifty years later, this may leave a lingering bitterness. 'You don't think I'd have married him if I didn't have to, do you?' was a not unusual private comment.

Indeed, given the widespread innocence about sexual matters and particularly about contraception and abortion, it is hardly surprising that 'shot-gun' marriages were not uncommon. A more cynical explanation cannot be totally discounted either: there were probably cases in which girls embarked on premarital pregnancies believing that a pregnancy would force the father into making a commitment and thus guarantee some sort of exit, if not immediately from home, at least from parental jurisdiction.

Few weddings in Lambeth in the years between the wars were the grand affairs described by the women's journals. The money was not around for anything like that. Sue Dexter's wedding was mundane.

> I got up in the morning and I left where I was working and I got on the tram and while I was on the tram a woman said to me 'Are you looking forward to getting married?' I didn't know this woman from Adam so I turned to her and I said 'How did you know I was going to get married?' She said 'I'm Fred's sister.' I'd never met any of his family and this is

how I met his elder sister, on the tram going to Walworth Road Registry Office!

And for Ada Terry,

When I got married, well, we never had such things as bands or pianos, or nothing. And you never had a hall, you had to have it in the house, in your back kitchen, the party, after they'd come home from the pub. There they were, all out the Queen's Head. I don't know where the beer come from. They might have fetched a few bottles home for indoors, but they'd all be singing and dancing in the road . . .

But the wedding day, however humble, marked the crossing from adolescence to womanhood. Thereafter young women were part of the married sorority, and entered into a different network of kinship relations and support.

Ignorance and poverty imposed severe strains on a marriage, as did overcrowding.

Sue Dexter:

After the wedding, we went to the pub and then Fred had to go back to work. So that was our honeymoon. I was going back to work, but on the night-time his mother said, 'You can't go back.' So I ended up staying with them. I'd never been to his house before. He wouldn't take me. He felt a bit ashamed because they were very poor. And I ended up sleeping with his sister and he slept with his brother, the same as usual. So we had no really first night, wedding night.

Then I found I was pregnant about six, seven weeks after the wedding. Nobody knows how it happened! We used to have our secret meetings, when nobody was there, you know, we used to make hay while the sun shone! But we hadn't had a lot of intercourse because we had to do it more or less secretly. I used to cringe up all the time in case somebody came and caught us. After we got a place of our own, we could make love at will.

Then the birth of the first child often entailed considerable stress for both parents. Financially, it meant the loss of the wife's earnings, and they had to make adjustments, to accommodate a baby within a relationship that was still new and raw, between two people who were very young.

In some cases the adjustment could not be made. Additional babies on an income that rarely increased, and in many cases decreased, within the same or similar space, resulted sometimes in a near breakdown of the relationship. 'I wasn't used to roughing it,' commented Sue, 'I felt that if I had to put up with that, I would have to leave him.' Or, as Fanny Abbott remarked, 'I do think there was a lot of knocking about in those days with men.' And Violet Harris told of her experiences:

I've had people coming to me when my husband's been walloping me up, dragged me out and take me in their house. Well, of course, you got it all the worse really when people interfered. When it was all done, you know, you'd get a punch in the clock for allowing that woman to come and interfere, see? You couldn't win. No, couldn't win. If you left your husband, who wants you with a big family of children? Nobody, do they? So you had to stick on. Never complained. Bash, bang, wallop. It was terrible, you know? Blooming hard life with him, and all. All those years were purgatory.

For women there was no way out. Divorce was beyond the financial, legal and moral reach of most women and, in any case, would not have guaranteed paternal maintenance.

Yet loyalty and hard work were sometimes considered adequate compensations. Marriage was also a means towards economic survival and the ability to provide or try to provide was an important quality in a husband. 'But he was a grafter, duck,' said Violet Harris.

And, clearly, many working-class marriages survived well and lovingly the material constraints and pressures imposed on them. 'No separations or divorces, or anything like that. We was a whole family,' remarked Nelly Brown, who was married to a market trader.

Just then, when you asked me about my hubby, well it chokes me when I think about that. How he came home from work one evening and I had some fish to fry for his supper, about nine o'clock. He shut up at eight o'clock most nights. Saturdays, eleven sometimes. And he came home and he said, 'I'm tired, girl. I'm going to bed. I'll have the fish for my breakfast.' Three days later he was dead. It chokes me when I think of it.

The sirens of war signalled formidable times. Life changed for the girls and women of Lambeth, as it did for everyone. Starting work at fourteen, just before the war, Viley Neal, for instance, earned

11s. 10d. [59p] a week when I started to the box-makers, George Harrods. My mum got the 10s [50p] and I got the 1s. 10d. [9p].

I often try to think back and remember how did we used to buy ourselves stockings, the old Bemberg, with the nice shaped back and heel, and ten cigarettes a week I used to buy, used to last me a week then . . .

Within a year or so, as the realities of living in a Britain threatened with invasion and subject to heavy bombing were faced, those ten cigarettes a week had increased to ten a day. Viley continued:

I was no hero. I really was frightened. Margie and I used to sleep in the kitchen downstairs in a chair bed, one each end. The rest of the house was empty, but we wouldn't go upstairs and we used to leave the Relay wireless on of a night because you'd hear a click in the night and that would wake you up and you'd hear, 'Enemy planes are crossing the coast.' Well, that used to give us time to get my mum out of bed and down the shelter before the actual warning went here.

One night I'm getting her over there and of course, with my hip, I couldn't run, she couldn't run because she was sort of paralysed down one side. She's holding my arm and we're trotting along and I could see this doodly bug up there, you know, oh God! The guns were going, I say to her, 'Don't panic, Mum, we're all right.' And when we gets to the shelter, they wouldn't let us down. They'd shut the gates. So I had to come from there and take her across to the Northern Line. How I never died of fright, I don't know. It's an awful experience when you think back on it. I was only grateful I never had any children, had I got married the early part of the war and had children, because it used to be terrible to see them run with the little kids.

I bought ten cigarettes a week till then. I smoked like a trooper from that night. I used to get five Weights on my way to work, and five Weights on my way home. They wouldn't let you have any more. And we get in and my dad would say 'Got your cigarettes today? Oh well, I got you ten Tenners.' They weren't very nice, but they were a cigarette.

The constant threat of tragedy forced maturity. Many young married women found themselves as single parents, in an atmosphere of fear and selfishness. Fanny Abbott suffered a tragic and unnecessary loss.

I lost a baby in the war. I fell on him. Up Schweppes's shelter. I went in there and all the clever boys, the desperadoes, as soon as the warning went, they all rushed, knocked me down the blinking stairs in Schweppes and I fell on the baby and hurt its chest. They couldn't get no motor to take us to St Thomas's, but someone come along and offered us a lift, a coal cart or something, took the baby there. They tried to feed him but it was just running out. I'd punctured, done something there. His name was Danny. Lovely curly hair. Cut his curls off and kept it in a bag. When they laid him in the cot in the ward, he was nearly five months, he was just beginning to know us and laughing and she laid him down and she said, 'You can sit with him a little while, the doctor's coming back.' Well, I'm sitting there and he kept opening his mouth. I said 'Look, he's got four teeth.' I didn't know he even had them. 'No,' she said, 'he's not smiling. It's the pain. Doctor says he can't do nothing else.' Of course, he just rolled and went and I'm saying, 'He's laughing, look.' Laid him down and they got a bit of wadding and the bandage and tied his face up, and I went potty, didn't I then?

Courtship under such conditions could not be anything other than intense. 'The war years' said Viley Neal, 'took a big lump out of our lives. My husband went in the Army at nineteen and came out at twenty-six. That's a long while.'

The unfamiliar constraints of war were added to the familiar ones of parental control, and leisure and pleasure were snatched where they could be found. Viley remembers:

Sometimes we'd venture out on Sunday, go over Hyde Park. I wasn't going out with my husband then, so we used to giggle around, get tangled up with Americans. They weren't my favourites, anyway, during the war. Very flash with their money and my friend and I, we had a bit of an argument with some of them. We was out on the boats, on the Serpentine there and because we just ignored them, they come close enough to take our oars off the boat, and off they went. We was just there! The bloke had to come and get us in. I suppose it had its funny side . . .

Rationing, clothing shortages and 'utility' fashion did much to take dress along the road of democracy; even make-up received official approval, as essential to the maintenance of morale. Such fashion as there was became closely allied to the war effort.

Between the wars clothes had been a means both of expressing sexuality and of disguising the ambiguity and ignorance surrounding it. Clothes had been a means of stating a distance from their parents, signifying an alternative to the overbearing poverty which stultified their imaginings. The models on offer may have been society's left-overs, but they were accessible. Although the war by no means smoothed over class differences, in dress it offered a uniformity of style and standard.

The young women who came to maturity after the war grew

up with images of women dressed, if not in uniform, at least uniformly. For the child such images would have been heavily masked by the reality of hard work and occasional tragedy. There was little of the glamour, of the daring of the previous decade. There was little of the celebration of womanhood which had also characterised the 1920s and 1930s. Most women had a uniform drabness about them, a frumpiness. The young women of the 1950s stood and observed their mothers, as their mothers had observed their own in the 1930s: as visually dull and sexually bland.

These young women were members of the first generation to benefit from major state aid, with its provision of health care, housing and income support and the governmental commitment to full employment and an adequate wage. This was accompanied by the visible reconstruction of their own city landscape.

Yet the perspective of the young girl in the 1950s was not so remarkably different from that of her mother. Whatever else was happening in a wider world of cultural and structural change, women's lives were not being fundamentally altered. The notion of marriage as the ultimate fulfilment of dreams and career was a notion with which both media and parents were in agreement. And still, squeezed between childhood and motherhood, was the black hole of maturity into which was sucked and randomly absorbed some of the conscious appraisals of the future woman.

But the images were changing. By the 1950s working-class fashion began to assume its own autonomy. At one extreme there were the Teddy boys and girls, dressed in a style that was a unique mix of Edwardian pastiche and contemporary American fashion. Tricia Dempsey described herself in her:

> . . . Teddy girl two-piece costume, it was a finger-tip drape, cut of the coat, and it cost me 13 guineas [£13.65] from Brixton market. It was a lot then. Took me six months to pay for it. And a flat beret. All the girls, all the Teddy girls, wore flat berets with a great big hat pin with a pearl in it, and string

pearls all tied up and that horrible pan-stick make-up, thick brown and great big thick lips, cerise pink, you know? You think of it now! That sickly pink!

The Teddy girls' mothers, in their heyday in the 1930s, had aimed at a style which mimicked haute couture, wearing clothes which had differed from those of their richer contemporaries only in their quality, not in their ideas or style. With the dress of the Teds, perhaps for the first time, high fashion for the working-class girl had become consciously and proudly specific, in a class, and age, of its own. Just as the old working-class areas were disappearing, cultural form began to express itself in dress.

By then the teenager had been invented; the period of growing up had been framed, defined as a commodity, and given its own distinctive livery. From the 1950s on, the idea of the teenager assumed a solid identity and a style of its own, a style which, for working-class girls, was uniquely about them, which had converted America to its own, and subverted older notions of 'smart'. Their images of the ideal woman were now based neither on the family nor on film, but on their immediate peers. The Teddy girl was one example. More common and more conventional was an image that emphasised sex in every contour, accentuating bust, waist, hips and legs. This woman had the figure of a seventeen-year-old, with bottom made to look large by the clinging lines of a cheap, tight skirt, and bust thrown forward by the effort of standing or walking on three-inch-high stiletto heels, the walk confined by the heels and the mean hemline measurement to no more than a 'mince', a 'wiggle and a walk'.

Young girls had money to spend, a direct consequence of the commitment to full employment and the developing service industries of central London. Tina Perkins was born in 1940 on the Duchy estate in Kennington where she still lives.

I was turned fifteen when I started the job, making transistor radios, and I used to get £2.10s. [£2.50] when I first started work. And I used to come home and used to give my mum

£1.10s. [1.50] of that, save 10s. [50p] a week pocket money and have the rest for my bus fare. That's how cheap it was . . .

And in recognition of their new spending power, teenagers were offered a range of commodities, including not only clothes but also, and especially, music and magazines. In the 1960s even the BBC reorganised its planning to cater for the teenage taste. More particularly, in the 1950s romantic comics aimed specifically at teenage girls began to appear. These comics (first cartoons and then photographic strips) were the heirs of an older tradition of pulp romantic fiction; but now they focused directly on the cohort of teenagers. Teenage meant maturity, and maturity meant falling in love. The theme was the same, but whereas before adolescent girls gazed on others, here they gazed on themselves. In the few and precious years which they had to grow up, marriage remained the end and sexuality the means. Even for a Teddy girl like Tricia Dempsey, the aim and culmination of youth was a slap-up wedding, a real picture postcard wedding, the stuff of fantasy.

One thing I always used to do (as a child), when we used to go over Lambeth Bridge there, to the park at Millbank, we'd walk over that bridge there and play at Lambeth Palace, on the corner there, the little church next to it, and it always had a pretty little garden. It's not as pretty now as it used to be. Roses, there was a little pagoda there, and I always used to lay there, round there and on the gravestones and that, and I always used to say, you'd say this if you went to the pictures, you know, 'Oh, the first dress that she wears will be mine, the second one will be yours.' All the Dorothy Lamours and all this, and I can always remember saying when we used to play at Lambeth Palace there, 'When I grow up I'm going to get married in this church' – this must have been during the war and just after – 'I'm going to get married in this church.' And I did, when I was nearly twenty-one. I said to myself, I love that church and though I'd never been inside it, I was going to get married in that church . . .

Those who benefited from post-war affluence had money available for conspicuous weddings for their daughters; and they were expected to spend it.

Carol Phillips was born in 1953 and lived in Vauxhall, first in a tenement house shared with her aunt and another family and then in a council flat. She still lives in Vauxhall with her husband and child, on the top floor of one of the few high-rise blocks in the area.

I was nineteen when I got married in the April. I don't know whether it was young, I think it depends on the individual, if you're mature enough to kind of face up to married life . . .

We got married in Caxton Hall and the reception was in the NAAFI hall, in Kennington Lane, because my father-in-law works for the NAAFI. It was a big wedding, a lot of money because I'm, you know, the only daughter. We had a sit-down meal for about a hundred and fifty people, and about four hundred on the night, I suppose. We got lots of really nice presents and everything. But it cost an awful lot of money. I mean, looking back, you think what you could have done with that money but there again I've got a daughter and I'd like for her to have exactly the same. I think it must have been very good because people still talk about it.

And after the wedding? The ideal of staying at home remained. Work had always been a stop-gap between school and marriage, and many girls were glad to 'pack it in' for the new experience of marriage. Tina Perkins:

I left when I got married, then it didn't matter. I just packed up and was a housewife after that, I never worked no more, until she was seven and I started back to work again.

Tina, like many others, looks back nostalgically to the brief period of youth before she married. Life for her as girl was, she said:

. . . quite exciting, real good fun we used to have, but then again I suppose I was only young and I used to come home from work, get dressed and go dancing, go to the Lyceum and all that. Them days used to be a laugh. Used to go away for weekends with some of the girls, we used to go down to the seaside. We used to have quite a good time. We used to go to coffee bars and just sit there drinking that espresso coffee, or go to the Hammersmith Palais. Then I was stupid, I went and got married. [And] I suppose all the rest I've been an old married woman. You have to go home and start cooking dinner and doing washing and everything else . . .

One of the most noticeable changes in Lambeth in recent years has been the increase in the number of single parents. For many girls, now, courtship leads not to marriage but directly to motherhood. The significance of this is discussed in more detail in Chapter 5, but an aspect worth noting here is the shift it indicates in girls' attitude to marriage. Certainly, although most working-class girls still live at home until marriage, it is clear that for a proportion of young women marriage no longer represents the only means of escape from home, or of establishing independence.

Yet there remains a contradiction between the romantic ideal and the reality of marriage which creates a conflict in the minds of many single parents. Karen Howard, for instance, protests:

I ain't married, no, I'm a single parent. Stay single, don't want to go and get married. I got two children, by the same dad. But we just can't get on. We're completely different. The only thing I regret now is meeting him. Don't regret having our kids, because I love my kids. I don't love him no more . . .

But for all she speaks of it with a wry cynicism, she still has a vision of 'the right man' as a saviour from without.

. . . Nice rich millionaire, out there somewhere. Some day my prince will come on his white horse. I'm still waiting for him, mate.

References
1. Maud Pember Reeves, *Round About a Pound a Week.*
2. *Titbits*, 2 January 1932.
3. *Woman's Own*, 15 October 1932.
4. *Titbits*, 9 January 1932.
5. See *New Survey of London Life and Labour*, 1934, and Slater and Woodside, *Patterns of Marriage*, 1951.

CHAPTER 5

Motherhood

. . . whatever the exact causes are which produce in each case the sickly children so common in these households, the all-embracing one is poverty. The proportion of the infantile death-rate of Hampstead to that of Hoxton – something like 18 to 140 – proves this to be a fact. The 42 families already investigated in this inquiry have had altogether 201 children, but 18 of these were either born dead or died within a few hours. Of the remaining 183 children of all ages, ranging from a week up to sixteen or seventeen years, 39 had died, or over one-fifth. Out of the 144 survivors 5 were actually deficient, while many were slow in intellect or unduly excitable. Those among them who were born during the investigation were, with one exception, normal, cosy, healthy babies, with good appetites, who slept and fed in the usual way. They did not, however, in spite of special efforts made on their behalf, fulfil their first promise. At one year of age their environment had put its mark upon them. Though superior to babies of their class who had not had special nourishment and care, they were vastly inferior to children of a better class who, though no finer or healthier at birth, had enjoyed proper conditions, and could therefore develop on sound and hygienic lines.[1]

Violet Harris suffered from malnutrition during the 1920s when her husband was out of work.

My husband [who was] a smart man . . . resorted to going round the streets selling tarry blocks, those blocks what they used to get out of the road years ago. Used to chop them up in bits, put them on the fire, bit cheaper than coal, you know? And he used to go round selling them, tuppence [1p] a pound for them. That was to get our rent, that money. And many a time I never got really a good meal. I always reckon, you know, being hungry was something to do with my Ada being born deficient . . .

Sue Dexter suffered it in the 1930s – and even after the Second World War she had

been in hospital with malnutrition. With six children to bring up, and my husband to look after, I always saw that they had enough to eat, and I would go without. He was only earning about £10 a week at Doulton's and even then, I mean the rent was £2.11s. [£2.55] here by then. He never knew, give him his due, he never knew I was going without, because he would say, 'Well, where's your dinner?' I'd say, 'Oh, I've had mine.' But I was lying because I didn't have enough to give them. I still do that, you know, now we're on the pension. I still do that. I would swear blind I've had my dinner and he doesn't know that sometimes I go without.

In 1915 in Lambeth as a whole 683 infants under one year died. The chief causes of death were 'debility, atrophy and inanition; congenital malformations, measles, whooping cough, bronchitis and other diseases of the respiratory organs, diarrhoea and prematurity.'[2] But the figures were higher in the inner wards of Marsh, Bishop's and Prince's.[3] In 1915, 20.3 per cent of deaths were of infants under five years old. In 1916, 290 new infants were entered on the registry and fed at the municipal milk depot, of whom 140 were described as 'below par constitutionally', 34 as 'weakly', 82 as 'wasting' and 34 as 'diseased'. In 1917, 198 new infants were fed, of whom 120 were described as 'below par but healthy', 9 as 'weakly', 53 as 'wasting' and 16 as 'diseased'. In 1918, 449 deaths of infants under one year were recorded.[4]

As Queenie Thomas recalled:

I mean, going to school lots of times you saw a little white coffin under the seat of the undertaker's. They used to be

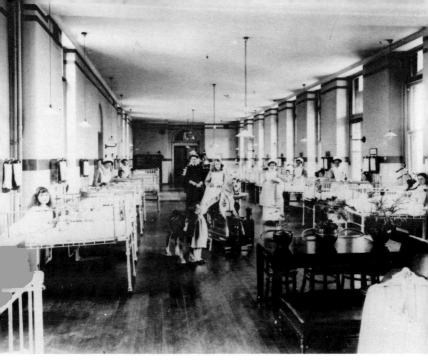

1 *Above*, The children's ward at the Royal Waterloo Hospital, 1913.

2 *Below*, Wickham Street, Vauxhall, 1914.

3 *Left above,* Schoolchildren outside the shops in Walnut Tree Walk, China Walk, 1929.

4 *Left,* Alleyway, Prince Buildings, 1930.

5 *Above,* Gym class in an unidentified evening school, early 1900s.

6 *Right,* Going-home time at Henry Fawcett School, Kennington, 1937.

7 *Left above*, China Walk Estate, 1934.

8 *Left*, China Walk Estate, 1940, after bomb damage, described simply as 'Incidents' at the time.

9 *Above*, Market stalls along The Cut, 1950.

10 *Right*, The Lambeth Baths, Lambeth Walk, 1975.

11 *Overleaf*, Lambeth street life, late 1940s.

12 *Left*, Children
gathered in the
Cowley Estate, 1972.

13 *Right*,
Housing near the
Elephant and
Castle, 1965.

having the adult in the back, you know, in a coffin, and this little white coffin used to be in the front because they died very young, didn't they? And they used to put them in the same grave as the adults, yeah. I've never seen a little white coffin for years. They used to be white silk outside. Yes. Of course, I love kids and it always used to affect me terrible. I used to go home, crying, you know?

In 1919 the Local Authorities Milk (Mothers and Children) order empowered Local Authorities to supply milk to expectant and nursing mothers and infants – a provision which was reduced in 1925 on the grounds of 'national economy'. These attempts to offer nutritional help and advice were piecemeal and inadequate. The root of the problem of ill health and poor nutrition was poverty. Not enough money came into the family to provide a consistently good diet or healthy housing.

The effects of malnutrition on maternal and infantile mortality were reflected unremittingly in the Medical Officer of Health's statistics. The mortality figures published in 1924, for instance, show that for the previous thirty years infantile mortality in the China Walk area had been significantly higher than that for the rest of the Borough – 136.5 as opposed to 113.8 per 1,000 registered births.[5]

In terms of general mortality this area of North Lambeth was significantly worse off than the rest. Death from diarrhoea, for instance, was almost double the Borough average (9.0 as opposed to 5.0) and that from tuberculosis (all forms) was similarly higher – 2.6 as opposed to 1.8. In the 1930s unemployment was gruesomely reflected in infant, neo-natal and maternal mortality. According to the *New Survey* infant mortality in Lambeth in 1930 was 60 per 1,000 births. In 1935, for the whole of the Borough, out of 3,823 registered births, there were 95 deaths of babies under one month, and 10 maternal deaths. Two hundred and twenty-five children under one year died. In the China Walk area, again, out of 619 births, 51 had died within a year; in Kennington, out of 652, 37 had died.[6]

In other words, almost one-third of Lambeth's infant and

neo-natal deaths occurred in the northern part of the Borough, where the worst unemployment was also found. In 1938, out of 3,846 births, there were 86 neo-natal deaths, 7 maternal deaths, and 196 infant deaths. One can assume that, again, the north of the Borough bore the brunt. The unemployment figures for those two years were comparable – 9,089 registered unemployed in 1935, 9,772 in 1938 (as opposed to 12,363 in 1932). One must remember also that maternal and neo-natal health is closely related to the health of the mother not only during pregnancy but also in the preceding years, including the mother's own history of childhood nutrition.

But although the infant and maternal mortality statistics are revealing, and provide a valuable indicator of both health and health-care standards between the wars, other factors have to be taken into account. Many maternal deaths were due to complications arising from abortion. Some abortions were carried out therapeutically, but many were criminal abortions. The Registrar General's returns in 1936 indicate that the vast majority of deaths from abortions were among married women. Most of them would have been working-class women who had either tried to induce the abortion themselves or had had it done on the cheap, and where the attendant risks would have been greater.

It was often the case that neither partner in a marriage had had any previous sexual experience or, indeed, had even the most rudimentary knowledge about sex.[7]

Sue Dexter:

He was a virgin as well. He'd never been with another girl – so we were both absolutely ignorant of anything like that, you know? It seems very, very funny now when we look at it, that we could be so ignorant but that's the way we were. He didn't know what to do when we got into bed, and I didn't know what to do – we just sort of fiddled around till we found something! This is awful! Obscene! But this is the way it was, you know?

The naïveness really amazed me after the first baby was

born. I thought, well, how stupid can you be. And even then I didn't know what was happening. I didn't, I really didn't. I didn't know where a baby came from. I thought they were going to cut me down here. I had no idea where a baby came from. I thought my stomach was going to burst open or they were going to cut me and take it out. And when it started coming from what I know now as the womb, I was really shocked. I really was shocked to think that a baby could come through there. There was no explanation given at all, and the nurses must have known that I was really ignorant. From then on I began to get a bit wiser! It was a wonder, a marvellous thing to me to think that the baby could come that way and it was a real eye-opener . . .

If knowledge of reproduction was limited, advice on contraception was even harder to come by. Evidence offered by Slater and Woodside suggests a widespread but unsystematic use of the most commonly available forms of contraception – the condom, *coitus interruptus* (withdrawal), or abortion.[8] And the oral evidence suggests a general ignorance – despite, or perhaps because of, the advertisements in the public lavatories (Gents only) indicating where 'letters' could be bought. 'They never had that then,' said Gracie Tarbuck. 'You had to have them [children] whether you wanted them or not. I said to my dad, I said, 'You'd better tie it up.'
Sue Dexter got similar advice from her mother-in-law.

I went to his mother when I knew I was having twins and I said, 'I don't know what I'm going to do. I'm having twins.' 'Well,' she said, 'the only thing you can do now is to put two legs in one stocking.' That was her contraception! If you put two legs in one stocking, he can't get at you! These were the sayings that all the people had because they didn't know anything.

Sue added:

. . . we didn't know anything about birth control. I didn't even till my kids got married. They taught me, honest truth.

I think I was naïve all my life, till my girls started growing up
and then talking to me about different things which amazed
me, because I didn't know the half of what went on.

With limited knowledge of contraception, abortion was
often the only way of limiting a family. Collecting figures on
abortion is notoriously difficult.[9] The successful ones for the
most part went undetected. Those that resulted in death had
clearly to be reported, but were not necessarily classified with
the maternal mortality figures; they might be categorised as
suicides or as deaths 'due to violence'. For instance, in 1933,
out of the 2,618 deaths during pregnancy, childbirth and the
puerperal state in England and Wales, 378 – or 14.4 per cent –
were attributed to criminal abortion but in addition another 85
deaths were assigned to various forms of violence, depending
on the coroner's verdict. Thus, 52 of these deaths were
assigned to suicide, 2 to murder, 6 to manslaughter, 1 to
offences against the person; in 24 cases an open verdict
was returned.[10] In Lambeth, the maternal mortality for 1934
was 13, of which only 10 are attributed to childbirth, and of
those 10 only 4 could be said definitely not to have been the
result of an attempted abortion.[11] Deaths reported as 'suicides'
or 'due to violence' would have been listed elsewhere and are
not differentiated or specified.

This year may be said to mark the beginning of a new phase
in our old struggle to win the Victories of Peace. So far our
work has shown us the great difficulties that lie in our way,
but we never despair of one day attaining our object: an
equal chance of health and strength for every Lambeth child.
    What makes the work more hopeful than in the past is on
the one hand the greater interest taken in matters of health
by all classes, and on the other the fact that the more
intelligent working-class woman is beginning to realise that
the conditions in which she finds herself are not pre-
ordained and unalterable. Our object is to teach her what to
want and how to get it.[12]

This extract is taken from the report of the Barley Mow Mothers' Institute for the year 1919–20. But although attendance at such clinics showed an increase (at the Barley Mow, for instance, attendance at clinics and classes more than doubled between 1914 and 1921), the facilities offered were no match for the prevailing social conditions. 'The root of many of our difficulties,' commented the same annual report, 'is still the housing question. The overcrowding, the small ill-ventilated rooms, the continual struggle against dirt and disease bred by dirt.'

Molly Nelson recalled:

Well, I had three Caesarians, I was too small-made to pass. And we had a little girl, God rest her soul, she only lived to twelve months. She had gastric enteritis. They're more advanced now with it. She was all right, then my landlady said, 'Molly, I don't like the look of her, run her up to the hospital.' Took her to Waterloo. I was sitting on the window ledge, outside the street door and a policeman come by. He says, 'Do you know the name of Emily, missus? I've been up and down looking for an hour.' He said, 'There's a little girl in Waterloo Hospital. You'd better go at once.' When I gets there, she's taking her last breath. I couldn't see her die. I never see her born and I never see her die. Chokes me.

By 1928 the relieving officer of the Lambeth Board of Guardians had begun to refer all cases of nursing or expectant mothers to the Lambeth maternity and child welfare centres. But this would only concern those who had applied for parish relief. There were still many families who, though unemployed, resisted parish relief and many in employment who were on, simply, starvation wages. Yet within the provision allowed Lambeth had done all it could. It had been one of the pioneers in offering milk provision and in establishing maternity and child welfare clinics and in acknowledging and co-operating with the voluntary agencies. By the 1920s efforts to improve the health of the inhabitants of Lambeth began to be concentrated on improving housing conditions. The annual reports of the Medical Officer of Health reflect this growing concern and shift in emphasis.

Even under the best conditions, having babies was difficult. Most were born at home. In 1924, of the 5,618 babies born in Lambeth, 3,915 were born at home,[13] usually under the supervision of a midwife or a doctor, or the kind of handy-woman described by Violet Harris.

> These people that used to follow up the doctor, like. They had to be well experienced so if the woman had that baby before the doctor arrived she could separate it, the mother see, and do the necessary, you know, clean it up and that. Or she'd leave it, they could leave it for an hour, but clean its eyes and mouth and that. But after that it was too dangerous, because of the afterbirth, see, so she could sever – do the naval cord and that. But she had to know.
>
> She used to do what I call my washing, nightdress and vest and that and the baby's washing, but no housework. I had to get on and all, you know? He had to do it when he come home or something like that. And look after the other children.

The remaining 1,703 births in 1924, were in institutions, a maternity home, a hospital or the Workhouse Infirmary.[14]

> All experience goes to show that ... there is a definite, deep-rooted prejudice in the minds of most people against the Workhouse Maternity Wards for confinements, as there is in connection with other Departments of Poor Law Administration. The same prejudice, though to a much lesser degree, is noticeable in connection with Lying-in Hospitals and the Maternity Departments of General Hospitals. Voluntary or Municipal Maternity Homes are preferred, and there is a widespread want for such semi-private institutions throughout the Borough of Lambeth.[15]

Sue Dexter had her first child in the Lambeth Hospital in 1935, not long after it had changed its name – if not its conditions – from the Workhouse Infirmary (Brook Drive):

It was very, very bad there. It was the worst birth I ever had really. I was left in the huge bare room with just a trestle table with a sheet over it. That was the delivery bed. We didn't have a proper delivery bed then, we just had this trestle table with a sheet over it and it was as hard as iron. It was right close up to a window and it was cold. It was January and it was bitterly cold out. I was shivering. I couldn't keep warm. I shall never forget that bed. And then when I finally called out that the baby was coming the nurse came in and she said, 'Oh no, you've got a while yet.' I mean, as a kid you get a bit frightened and you're having your first baby. I was twenty and, I mean, in this day twenty would be more grown-up than I was at twenty. They left me hour after hour.

I think it was quite a long labour because it started early in the morning and it must have been about two o'clock in the afternoon when I had the baby and I looked out of the window and the first thing I knew was, I said, 'Oh, it's snowing', and then I think I passed out, I just couldn't – I was either too tired or too worn out I suppose.

And next thing I knew I was in a bed in a ward along horrible wooden floors, all spiky and all splinters. Oh, it was really terrible. A high iron bed, well, they still are, but it was very uncomfortable and you didn't have your babies with you. The babies were brought in at feeding times. And then I asked for something to eat and they said, 'Oh, you can't have anything to eat for the first two days.' You never got anything to eat for the first two days, only hot drinks. You weren't allowed anything.

I hadn't had a good meal in I don't know how long and I was looking forward to something. No, they never gave you anything to eat at all. Just hot milk or tea.

Choice of birthplace often followed the ebbs and flows of the family's finances. This was the experience of Violet Harris.

I had my first one, a stillbirth, during the First World War. Fred – of course, I'd been working and had a few pound by me then so he was all right, had him in a nursing home. My

Gladys I had in Tyers Street, [at] my Aunt Polly's. Well, then I had Henry in Lambeth Infirmary, Lena I had at home, Ada I had at home and Dulsie I had at home.

Home births were usually less a preference than the result of Hobson's choice for those unable to pay for private attendance and unwilling to enter into an institution unless they were destitute. The conditions for home births were rarely conducive to health: as the Lambeth Medical Officer of Health pointed out, the home was generally unsuitable, and, 'in the majority of cases, overcrowded . . . Peace and quiet are all essential for expectant mothers during their confinements'.[16] Peace and quiet were easier to prescribe than to provide, however, as Violet Harris explains.

When I had my Lena, I had to have the other poor little darling – was no age – on the bed with me all day, you know, crying. There was this other little one . . . getting more notice than a tiny born baby . . . used to look in their heads, on the bed, you know, see there was nothing in them . . .

But there was no mess at home, or nothing, see. I didn't have a proper convenience. All I had to do, you know, in a chamber or pail or something, you know. Put under me. Because you wasn't allowed to get out of bed, not even to have your bed made, for seven days. And then you were got up on the tenth, or eleventh day and then you went out on the twelfth day, you know, to be churched and then on the fourteenth day, like, you had the baby christened, usually, if you was all right . . .

It was precisely at these points that family and neighbours stepped in, lending clothes and practical support until the mother was able to look after the family again. But a new-born baby necessarily involved a considerable amount of work which had to be taken on in addition to the normal household duties. Without the benefit of plastic or even rubber knickers and sheets, the mothers were, according to Violet again:

. . . everlasting changing the kid. They used to have a belly binder, you know. It was a hard, rough stuff on, like huckaback. Well, then, over that, the first binder, there was a flannel one all over the little navel, like and that. The next one was a long white – what they used to call back flannel, made of flannelette, warm, you know and that used to be put over like that and done up with two pins, see, to keep their little feet warm. Well, then, over the back used to come this here, what we called a stiff binder, it was to keep the back straight and then on top of that used to be the bedgown, nightgown, see, and then a little matinée coat. The napkins, well my mum used to give me the tails of my dad's old shirts to make up into napkins. Course, we used so many, see? We used to hold the baby out a bit, and that, used to hold it out, like, to go its business from quite a young, little baby, you know?

I breast-fed all mine. Each one of them. But even so they hadn't got the napkin on, I suppose, about a quarter of an hour, half an hour, and it was soaking right through, the upper clothes and all. We hadn't got no rubber knickers, dear, no. I think, up to about Ada I think it was that the rubber knickers started, and they weren't nice, darling. They used to hold the water, you know. Nasty. No, you had to be very careful because of the child getting chafed from that, what they call a nappy rash bottom. Now, today, they've got everything, haven't they? I mean, we had no washing machine, we had no nothing, no nothing at all.

Everlasting changing, everlasting washing, with little space for either and even less for drying the baby's – and younger children's – wet clothes. Keeping the baby warm in winter was also a problem, as Sal Beckford described:

Couple of wool shawls, couple of matinée, big matinée whatsernames, you know. Course, didn't go out much in the winter, kept mostly warm indoors with a bit of fire, you know? I always had a nice big shawl. One of the shawls you used to like to keep as you took it out, you know, so it always looked smart, put it all on the pram, see. Never got no blooming pram covers like they do now, no big plush woolly things, just a bit of clean blanket, you know?

A new pram was clearly way beyond the financial scope of most Lambeth families. In 1928 the 'Marmet Baby Carriage' cost 5 guineas (£5.25); the 'Graves Baby Carriage' cost £3.10s. (£3.50), or 7s. (35p) down and 7s. monthly. Dole money, in 1931, was set at a minimum rate of 15s.3d. (76p) for a man over twenty-one; additional claims could be made for dependents. Many men even in full employment would not have earned substantially more. Prams were one of the many commodities which would have been acquired second-, third- or fifth-hand.

The requirements of a new baby generally sharpened the need to recycle goods. Many mothers showed great ingenuity. Tricia Dempsey remembered how:

> Me mum paid 6d. [2½p] for an orange box from a green-grocer's – this must have been in the war – and she painted it and stood it on its side and that was the baby's little cupboard, you know, that you put your powder and oils in and that ... I can also remember me mum buying from McDougall's, I think it was, along the Embankment, the Albert Embankment, the flour factory, you could buy – I suppose they were torn or ripped or something – old flour bags and they were very, very soft, and me mum would restitch them for pillow slips. They managed and scratched through.

A new-born would generally have some sort of makeshift cot – perhaps made from an old drawer – until it was old enough to move into a bed shared with older brothers and sisters. Occasionally, the baby shared the parental bed. But with no protective clothing available, such sharings must have been sodden affairs for all concerned, adding to the general discomfort, and the difficulty of keeping warm during the winter months.

The problems of poverty and poor nutrition were brought sharply into focus again with the economic depression of the 1930s.

Under the old system of parish relief, assistance was offered in kind, as Violet Harris described.

> They used to give you what they called parish relief, served it out on the premises, along the Kennington Lane, right opposite the police station there. They used to give you some meat, black as your hat. True. Potatoes, with whiskers all growing out of them. Black sugar. Black, almost, bread. Yards of treacle and blooming old car grease supposed to be margarine, you know. But you never got a penny off of them. You had to get that money, as best way you could, see, for the rent.
>
> We really almost survived on the old tripe they was giving us, like the black meat. When it was dark one night, I came out of bed and there was this like shining, in the dark, like a load of phosphorous on the meat. There!

It was often private philanthropy which came to the rescue of a starving and near-destitute family. Kitty Barnet described the calculated way in which:

> My dad became a Salvation Army man and he said that it was the only way he could get anything to wear. He got a uniform. And then me and my three sisters became Sunbeams and we had a little grey uniform with red piping. I've never worn that colour since. With a little pudding hat, you know, and of course we all got a dress then. That was the only way my dad used to be able to get any clothes.

And Gracie Tarbuck remembers with affection that

> . . . there used to be a lot of good things going on or else we'd never have managed. There was a lot of good things going on where you could get help. There was a convent that we had near us that was ever so good. Those nuns, they'd never, if you went and knocked at their door and said, 'We haven't any dinner', you'd go in and they'd give you something to eat. They used to go round in twos and if they saw a little

child they'd go and say, 'Have you had your dinner today?'
Really, and they'd take them and give them something to eat.
We got up one Sunday morning and all as we had was a
packet of Quaker Oats you know, and that was on a Sunday.
My mum went out and she was crying. My dad thought she
was going to do herself in like because we was in such a bad
way. But if it hadn't been for those nuns we would really
have been without, you know? But they came and gave my
father and all of us and put the dinner there and my mum, all
that she could do was cry . . .

The canny could, and did, travel afar to get the maximum
leverage out of the minimum conditions, as Gladys Harman
recalled:

Every week on a Friday night all the kids used to get together
and go in Shaftesbury Hall, down Great Dover Street. And
that's where all the children used to go there and they'd get,
perhaps, sometimes, they'd bring you a bit of fish on a lump
of bread, anything like that. You always got something. And
regularly the kids all got together and said, 'Come on, Friday
night, go up to Shaftesbury Hall . . .'

Soup kitchens were part of many children's gastronomic
tours. Ada Terry described how they would go to:

Lambeth Baths, to have this here dinner. All lined up in this
great big hall, tables laid out with soup bowls and this boy,
this boy was sitting near my brother. Of course, we were
going to have a prayer, see, first, grace. This boy knew my
brother and he was whispering to him. All of a sudden 'Oi!'
This old girl's got a great big chain round her neck with a
policeman's whistle on it. ''Ere' she says 'stop talking!'

And Maude Springer remembered that:

When I was at school I used to have a ticket and I used to go
through the park opposite St Thomas's Hospital and there
used to be a place there where you could go and get soup and
a lump of bread . . . My brother used to have half a pint of
milk a day.

But then, as Ada Terry recalled,

> Everything we did was for grub because, I mean, we was all
> half starved. Never got a cup of tea. A cup of tea went
> between you, a saucerful each. Can't afford a cup. In fact, I
> don't think we had that many cups, see. 'Here y'are, there's
> your saucer.'

It is true that by 1938 the School Medical Officer for the
London County Council could report optimistically that
between 1905-12 and 1938 London schoolchildren had, on
average, shown an increase in height for boys of 5.6 cm, and for
girls of 5.4 cm and had shown an increase in weight of 3.4 kg
for boys and 3.7 kg for girls. 'Compared with English children
generally, London children have shown an improvement in
physique greater than, on average, English children.'[17]
But this improvement indicated an average only. Broken
down by representative boroughs, this report also showed that
children from the better boroughs had shown an excess in
improved height and weight over those from poorer boroughs.

> The standard of nutrition [wrote Dr Priestley, Lam-
> beth's Medical Officer of Health] of Lambeth children
> on entering the County Council Schools is of interest
> when read in conjunction with the unemployment
> figures.

| | 1932 – 3,606 children | | | 1933 – 3,409 children | | |
	Good	Average	Below Normal	Good	Average	Below Normal
Children	867	2,528	210	733	2,431	244
Lambeth	24%	70.2%	5.8%	21.5%	71.3%	7.2%
London	22%	73.5%	4.5%	20.5%	75.4%	4.1%

| | 1934 – 3,210 children | | | 1935 – 3,388 children | | |
	Good	Average	Below Normal	Good	Average	Below Normal
Children	622	2,363	225	587	2,430	362
Lambeth	19.4%	73.6%	7.0%	17.3%	71.7%	11.0%
London	20%	75.9%	4.1%	16.4%	77.9%	5.7%[18]

Those children entering school in 1935 would have been born and spent their early years during the period of highest unemployment. Insufficient income meant poor food and inadequate housing. The correlation between social conditions and health and welfare appeared as irrefutable in the 1930s as it had to Booth at the turn of the century and to Maud Pember Reeves in 1913. The number of deaths of children under one year confirmed this. In 1936, 230 infants died in Lambeth, compared with 163 in the far wealthier borough of Kensington. Live births for that year in Lambeth were 3,871 and in Kensington 2,228.[19]

The series of twice-yearly measurements on London schoolchildren which was inaugurated in 1935 by Sir Frederick Menzies, the School Medical Officer, was discontinued in 1952. These measurements had been intended to supervise the nutritional conditions of children and to select those requiring special investigation and, if necessary, provide them with milk, cod liver oil and school meals. By 1952 it was becoming clear, as the London County Council *Report on the Heights and Weights of School Pupils in the County of London in 1959* pointed out, that, in the previous decade, not only had the average increase in height and weight reached what appeared to be a stable level but also regional differences between height and weight had diminished. Moreover, nationally, infant mortality had shown a sharp decrease. In the first fifty years of the twentieth century the infant mortality rate had been reduced from one in six at the turn of the century, to one in thirty-three in 1951.[20]

It was a time of congratulation. Before the war, by far the smallest of London's children had been found living in the poorest areas – north and south of the Thames from Westminster to the Docks. The social conditions which had prevailed in these areas had been dramatically improved and were being reflected in the health of the schoolchild. In Britain generally the post-war emphasis on health and the centralisation and improvement in social and welfare benefits had brought about a healthier nation.

The health of the Borough – wrote Lambeth's Medical Officer of Health in 1949 – . . . has not suffered in the least as the result of the transfer of services[21] which, considering the extent of the change, is a good augury for the future. The population has increased by roughly 3,000 and at 226,000 is well above the number 215,00 envisaged in the County of London Plan. Both the birth rate and the death rate have fallen, maternal mortality is down almost to vanishing point at 0.23, while the infantile mortality at 27 shows in dramatic fashion how times have changed since the temporary female health visitor was appointed in 1906.[22]

Statistics such as those used by the Board of Inland Revenue[23] appeared to confirm this optimism; inequality in post-war Britain was being ironed out as pre-tax incomes were being levelled up. Under such conditions no one, not even those at the lowest end of the social scale, living on National Assistance, had the excuse, or right, to be poor. And, indeed, with free school milk and meals, no child could or should be undernourished or malnourished.

Throughout the 1960s the School Health Service Reports for Lambeth continued to endorse the picture that the health of the children was being maintained.

The general health of schoolchildren remains good . . . the only rising figure is that of children referred by school medical officers to special investigation centres, 228 new cases in 1967 compared with 185 in 1966. This increase is due to enuresis. Strong contributory causes in enuresis are poor training and poor housing conditions. There is no evidence of an increase in poor health.[24]

However, there was some evidence to contradict the confidence that inequality and all that it implied was being eroded.[25] Even the Registrar General had pointed out in 1951 that infant mortality was about two and a half times greater in social class V than in social class I.[26] Studies of poverty indicated that not only old people – a predictably vulnerable category – but, more significantly, children also were still at risk from poverty.

> For over a decade it has been generally assumed that such poverty as exists is found overwhelmingly among the aged. Unfortunately it has not been possible to estimate from the data used in this study exactly how many persons over minimum pensionable age were to be found among the 7½ million persons with low income in 1960. However, such data as we have suggest that the number may be around 3 million. There were thus more people who were not aged than were aged among the poor households of 1960. We have estimated earlier that there were about *2¼ million children in low income households in 1960. Thus quantitatively the problem of poverty among children is more than two-thirds of the size of poverty among the aged* (my italics).[27]

Between 1953–4 and 1960, the estimated total of people in Britain living below the poverty line (calculated as the basic assistance level) had increased from approximately 600,000 to 2,000,000, of whom a significant proportion were children.[28] In 1981 the Department of Health and Social Security official figures indicated that 7,750,000 people were living at or below the supplementary benefit level. Although the latest figures are unavailable, calculations taking into account the increase in unemployment and cuts in unemployment benefit would suggest that there are at least 9,000,000 people living in poverty.

In 1981 the largest category in the poverty league consisted of those on low pay, swiftly followed by the unemployed and single-parent households. Thirty-five per cent of all adults in poverty were there as a result of low pay, 33 per cent because of unemployment. In other words, by far the greatest number of those living at or below the poverty line were in households of people of working age, many of them with family responsibilities. It has been calculated that in 1983 2,500,000 children were living in poverty.

One crucial indicator of poverty is found in nutritional standards. The National Food Survey, which was started in the 1950s, demonstrated that throughout the 1950s and 1960s the narrowing of inequalities in nutritional standards was maintained. When examined closely, however, this could be seen to be the result of improvements among certain sectors of the population, such as old age pensioners. There had been little overall improvement, and, indeed, for some sectors of the population, such as families on low income, there had been a deterioration. In 1960, it was reported:

> In terms of an analysis by family size, there are now more segments of the population below the BMA standard and for more nutrients than in 1950. As far as the numbers of population are concerned, the indications are that at least a quarter and possibly a third of the people of Britain live in households which fail to attain all the desirable levels of dietary intake. And, contrary to what is so often believed, the numbers in this situation seem to have increased since the mid-fifties.[29]

One of the difficulties in dealing with questions of nutrition is that there is some dispute as to what should be the recommended nutrient intake: for example, the United States National Research Council offers different and higher standards than those of the British Medical Association, while the BMA's standards are higher than those laid down by the National Food Survey Committee. At the same time, any recommended level provides only a crude measure, as requirements vary considerably from person to person. Research in this area has so far been inadequate, and:

> Until such work is done, uncertainty as to the precise nature of the position will remain and with it not only the inability adequately to isolate and deal with potentially vulnerable groups but also perhaps an overreadiness to discount any suggestion of malnutrition.[30]

Moreover, as Peter Townsend suggests, some of the 'more disturbing' findings on nutritional levels, particularly among children, have not been fully published – although, for instance, a scatter diagram at the end of *A Nutrition Survey of Pre-School Children 1967–68*, published by the Department of Health and Social Security, 'clearly showed that a very large number of children had less than 80 per cent of the recommended daily energy intakes.'[31]

There is therefore a problem in correlating information on poverty and nutrition. Specifically, it has not been possible to obtain figures on poverty and nutrition in Lambeth. Nevertheless, there is no doubt that there is a relationship between poverty, diet and health, and that this relationship not only affects the healthy development of the child, but will also influence the health of subsequent generations. And since unemployment in North Lambeth is higher than the national average, and many families in the borough live on social security or supplementary benefit, it is not unreasonable to suspect that many children in North Lambeth are living on or below the poverty line – and that many may well be suffering from low nutritional levels or actual malnutrition.

The nutritional status of children is influenced by the mother's diet and nutritional status even before conception. But, in particular, a mother's diet in pregnancy is a very important factor in determining the health and the size of her baby. Pregnant women and women who are breast-feeding have high dietary requirements. In *Poverty and Pregnancy*, the results of a survey carried out by the Maternity Alliance and published in 1984, it was estimated that an 'adequate' diet for two adults living on supplementary benefit would have taken approximately 9–10 per cent of their income (excluding housing), while to provide an adequate diet for a pregnant woman 28 per cent of that income would have had to be spent on food.[32] The survey revealed that out of the sample of 30 women whose husbands were unemployed, 18 indicated that they had difficulty in affording an adequate diet.[33]

Karen Howard, who is a single parent bringing up her two

young children on supplementary benefit, gave the following account of the birth of her second child.

> They told me to come in, they said they think the baby's small, they can't understand why, because I had a couple of weeks to go only, and I could see the consultant, and my blood pressure was 190 over something . . . they put me on a heart monitor machine. I said to them, 'Why are you doing it?' 'Oh, we're just watching your blood pressure.' But I knew that was a heart machine. I thought, no, there's something wrong here. There was about four nurses and you don't have that round you when you're having your second baby, and I couldn't understand why . . .
>
> They gave him all these tests. He was screaming. I had to go – I was in hysterics – I was walking up and down the corridor, I was crying. I didn't know what to do . . . Well, what do you do when they tell you something's wrong with your baby's heart . . . My first baby (when I was working), he was healthy, he was fat.

In Lambeth in 1985, the number of stillbirths was 27, the same as it had been in 1949 (although the population of Lambeth in 1985 was larger than that in 1949), while the proportion of babies weighing less than 2,500 grams was significantly higher, at 8.6, than the national average of 7.8.[34] Indeed, since the war, although there has been improvement in Lambeth's rate of infant mortality, the improvement is not as great as that in, for instance, Kensington and Chelsea. (Kensington was the area chosen for comparison with Lambeth by Maud Pember Reeves in 1913.) In 1951 the total number of stillbirths was 81 in Lambeth (population: 226,200), 48 in Kensington (population: 170,600).[35] In 1981 there were 29 stillbirths in Lambeth (population: 256,200), 11 in Kensington and Chelsea (population: 146,900).[36] In 1985 the number of stillbirths was 27 in Lambeth (population: 243,500), 5 in Kensington, (population: 137,600).[37] The perinatal mortality rate was 11.9 for Lambeth, 6.1 for Kensington and Chelsea.[38]

Young children are very vulnerable to deprivation. Deirdre

Patel describes the following experience, which occurred while she was living on supplementary benefit.

> Nita was under the hospital for two years because she had a fit on me. They couldn't figure out what it was. She was a year and a half, and she was – because of her weight – I was sitting down and all of a sudden I looked over and I thought it was like froth coming out of her mouth. She went all blue . . . wasn't even breathing . . . got on the phone. I said, 'The baby's dead! The baby's dead!' I was lucky, the doctor was downstairs and he came up. She was in for two months. They gave her the all-clear. They said she's getting taller now so they're not worried, but her weight – she's not even two stone, this one . . .

The correlation between family poverty and the lower than average height and weight of children shows a consistent trend.[39] Children of unemployed fathers are, on average, shorter than those of the employed and, at most ages, boys and girls whose fathers are manual workers are shorter than those whose fathers are in non-manual employment.

Children receiving free school meals have a poorer nutritional state than other children, a difference accounted for by the degree of poverty in the children's families.[40] And welfare policy concerning the provision of school milk and free school meals was changed in 1971, despite fifty years of evidence that such provision benefited the most deprived children.[41]

One of the major factors in poverty for many of the mothers in Lambeth now is single parenthood. Indeed, this is the most important demographic change, signalling a significant shift not only in attitudes, but also in the causes and consequences of poverty, with both short- and long-term implications for maternal and child health and welfare.

By the 1970s illegitimacy generally no longer bore the stigma which it had, for both mother and child, before the Second World War. And in Lambeth the influence of different ethnic cultures, particularly West Indian, had merged with a broader increase in sexual permissiveness to create a situation where sexual relations before marriage were both permitted and expected, and where pregnancy did not necessarily force the parents into a marriage based on 'doing the decent thing'. Similarly, divorce had become more socially acceptable. And after the Divorce Reform Act of 1971, divorces were easier to get, and did not require costly and embarrassing 'proof'.

But there is also a class dimension to single parenthood. Both the highest illegitimacy rates and the highest divorce rates are to be found among those in social class V.

By 1981 single-parent households made up approximately 10 per cent of households in Lambeth.[42] The average of single-parent households throughout Lambeth's council estates stood at 14 per cent, and on the Kennington Park and Tanswell estates, the percentage stood at 20 per cent.[43] By 1985 Lambeth had the highest illegitimacy ratio in the country. In England and Wales as a whole the ratio was 192 to 1,000 live births. In Lambeth it was 430 per 1,000.[44] In 1985, in Lambeth, there were 2,292 legitimate and 1,728 illegitimate births.[45] The proportion of illegitimate births has been rising steadily since 1951, as the following table demonstrates:

	Population	Legitimate births	Illegitimate births
1936	279,900	3,617	254
1946	209,910	4,395	398
1951	226,200	3,550	279
1961	221,960	4,132	776
1971	304,410	4,258	1,017
1974	295,300	3,024	861
1980	256,200	2,554	1,225
1985	243,500	2,292	1,728[46]

Most girls who found themselves pregnant in the period between the wars married the father. In Slater and Woodside's survey 8 out of 200 women admitted to being pregnant at the time of their marriage but, as the authors observe, 'there were probably others who did not report it.'[47] Certainly, nationally, 70.2 per cent of extra-maritally conceived pregnancies in 1938 were subsequently legitimated by the marriage of the parents before the birth of the child, whereas in 1961 only 57.9 were subsequently so legitimated.[48]

Of the pregnant girls who did not marry, it seems that many, perhaps the majority, continued to live with their parents. At an official level the family was certainly encouraged to support their 'fallen' offspring. In 1946, for instance, the Southwark Diocesan Association for Moral Welfare received a grant from Lambeth which assisted 125 unmarried mothers and their children and 40 unmarried expectant mothers from Lambeth.

> As a result of the efforts of the Welfare visitors, no less than 71 girls were able to return home with their babies, which is the best solution of the difficulty. Of the rest, 7 babies were cared for by foster mothers, 15 went to residential nurseries, places were found for 6 in day nurseries while the mother went out to work and provided a home out of nursery hours, 15 were adopted, 6 mothers found homes with friends for themselves and their babies. The remaining 5 babies did not survive the year.[49]

This clearly does not represent the total of illegitimate children (398 were born in Lambeth in 1946), but it is indicative of attitudes towards the welfare of mother and child. The desired solution, for the mother to remain within her parents' home, was also the preferred one for many of the women themselves – despite the often appalling overcrowding.

The incidence of single parenthood in the years between the wars was perhaps not quite as low as official statistics indicate. There is some evidence that illegitimacy could be 'hidden' within the family, and though divorce was out of the question for most working-class men and women, separation may have occurred more frequently than was admitted. Nevertheless, there has certainly been a significant shift in patterns of child rearing, which suggests a shift in attitudes, in recent years –

f Lambeth, *Annual Report of the Medical Officer of Health*,

Gittins, *The Family in Question*, 1985.
Whitehead, *The Health Divide*, Health Education Council,

though it could be argued that a higher incidence of single parenthood and illegitimacy is no more than a reversion to much older patterns of relationships in working-class communities.[50] The 1983 illegitimacy rate of 22.4 per 1,000 live births was the highest since 1861, when it stood at 18 per 1,000.

The interplay between poverty and ill health represents a vortex into which the poor are consistently sucked. Ill health both causes unemployment and can be seen as the result of unemployment.[51] And material deprivation results in physical deterioration and great mental strain. GP consultation rates are significantly higher for women in social classes IV and V than for those in classes I, II and III.[52] In the Maternity Alliance survey published as *Poverty and Pregnancy* stress and tension was mentioned by one mother in three, and studies reported in *The Health Divide* concluded that working-class women living in urban areas ran a very high risk of depression.[52]

Stress, tension and depression are all debilitating sicknesses. At its most extreme, depression can lead to suicide. Stress and tension result in a profound weariness, disturbed sleep, irritability and an inability to 'cope' which, in turn, aggravates the stress. With no prospect of alleviating the causes, which are too often social rather than physiological, the symptoms multiply.

As Karen Howard put it, 'It's all coming out, now, you know, all these illnesses and that . . .' And Deirdre Patel,

> I get very depressed sometimes. I was bad a couple of years ago, I was really bad. I felt so depressed and closed in here. I felt I was going to finish myself. I was in a total – I don't know what it was, I was so frightened I was going to harm the kids. That's how depressed I got . . .

References

1. Maud Pember Reeves, *Round About a Pound a Week*.
2. *St Thomas's Hospital Reports*, 'Report of the Out-patient Obstetrical Department', 1928.
3. Borough of Lambeth, *Annual Report of the Medical Officer of Health*, 1916.
4. Ibid., 1918.
5. Total averages 1895–1924, ibid., 1924.
6. Ibid., 1935.
7. According to Eliot Slater and Moya Woodside, *Patterns of Marriage* (1951), 36 per cent of the men and 50 per cent of the women claimed that they had had no sex relations, with the eventual spouse or others, before marriage.
8. Slater and Woodside, ibid.
9. See, for instance, Mary Chamberlain, *Old Wives' Tales*, Virago, London, 1981.
10. *The Registrar General's Statistical Review for England and Wales 1933*, HMSO, London, 1935.
11. Borough of Lambeth, *Annual Report of the Medical Officer of Health*, 1934.
12. *Annual Report of the Mothers' Institute 'Barley Mow'*, 1919–20.
13. Borough of Lambeth, *Annual Report of the Medical Officer of Health*, 1924.
14. Ibid.
15. Ibid., Appendix Three, 'Maternity Needs of the Borough of Lambeth'.
16. Ibid.
17. London County Council, *Report by the School Medical Officer on the Average Heights and Weights of Elementary School Children in the County of London*, 1938.
18. Borough of Lambeth, *Annual Report of the Medical Officer of Health*, 1935.
19. *The Registrar General's Statistical Review for England and Wales 1936*, HMSO, London, 1938.
20. Ibid. 1951, HMSO, London, 1954.
21. The National Health Service Act 1946 transferred the responsibilities of the local authorities for hospitals and some of the provisions of local sanitary authorities to the newly created local health authorities.
22. Borough of Lambeth, *Annual Report of the Medical Officer of Health*, June 1949.
23. Board of Inland Revenue, *92nd Annual Report*, HMSO, London, 1950. See R. M. Titmuss, *Income Distribution and Social Change* (1962) for a detailed critique of such statistics; also, Peter Townsend, *Poverty in the United Kingdom*, 1979.
24. Inner London Education Authority, *School Health Service Report*, 1967–68.
25. Peter Townsend, op. c
26. *The Dicennial Suppleme* London, 1951.
27. Brian Abel-Smith and
28. Ibid.
29. R. Lambert, *Nutrition i* Townsend, op. cit.
30. J. C. McKenzie, 'Poverty *of Poverty*, ed. Peter Townsend
31. See also *Annual Report of t* London, 1966.
32. L. Durwood, *Poverty and P*
33. Ibid.
34. *Mortality Statistics, Perinat* series DH3 no. 18, OPCS, 1985
35. *The Registrar General's Sta* HMSO, London, 1954.
36. *Local Authority Vital Statistic*
37. *Population and Vital Statistics.* series VS no. 12, PP1 no. 8, OPCS
38. Ibid.
39. R. J. Rona, A. V. Swan and D Gain of Primary Schoolchildren *Epidemiology and Community Medicin*
40. R. J. Rona, S. Chinn and A. Growth of Primary Schoolchildren' *Health*, no. 37, 1983.
41. See H. C. Corry-Man, 'Diet fo *Research Council Special Report*, seri which suggested that one pint of mi substantially higher growth rates amo et al., 'School Milk and Growth in 1978, which also indicated that girls i supplement.
42. London Borough of Lambeth, 1981.
43. London Borough of Lambeth, *E*
44. *Population and Vital Statistics: Loc* series VS no. 12, PP1 no. 8, OPCS, 19
45. Ibid.
46. Based on *The Registrar General's S* for the relevant years.
47. Slater and Woodside, op. cit.
48. *The Registrar General's Statistical I* HMSO, London, 1964.

49. Borough
1946.
50. See Dian
51. Margaret London, 1987.
52. Ibid.
53. Ibid.

CHAPTER 6

Keeping House

When it comes to a pinch, food is the elastic item. Rent is occasionally not paid at all during a crisis, but the knowledge that it is mounting up, and that eventually it must be paid, keeps these steady folk from that expedient save as the last resource. A little less food all round, though a disagreeable experience, leaves no bill in shillings and pence to be paid afterwards. Down to a certain low minimum, therefore, food may sink before leaving the rent unpaid, or before pawning begins.[1]

Between the wars, survival meant the ability to live off the neighbourhood.

Shopping was more complicated than the simple laws of supply and demand would suggest. It required time, effort – and ingenuity. Above all, it involved some highly creative accounting: short of cash, and denied credit, ways had to be found of meeting the shortfall between income and expenditure.

Casual labour was one such way. Between the wars, many women with young families could not take on regular employment. They did not have the time, and many employers discriminated against married women. Equally, many men did not like the idea of their wives going out to work. But there was seasonal work, such as pea-shelling in Covent Garden, or further afield, and with the whole family, hop-picking in Kent. There was also outwork, in the garment and related trades. There was other kinds of home work, such as washing and ironing. There was cleaning work, or work as a street vendor. Casual labour, especially if done at home, was a means of keeping the wolf at bay, and maintaining face. But it was not always available, or always sufficient.

The most common way of raising extra funds was through converting consumables – goods – into cash, entering into the sub-economy. The market exchanged cash for consumables: the sub-economy converted those consumables back into cash. Indeed, the creation of such an economy was under-emphasised in Pember Reeves's account, for it implied an improvidence on the part of the poor.

At its most extreme, housing was a commodity which could be traded. Money and time could be bought by delaying the rent. Although the final cost could be eviction, even this was sometimes evaded by a 'moonlight flit'. More commonly rooms were traded, from front to back, from up to down. Where and what you traded matched the family fortunes and aspirations. How well you traded reflected the ingenuity of the mother, for it was her skills and her reputation that secured the best housing accommodation, retained existing accommodation when the family fell on hard times, or used the accommodation to generate income from subletting. Although the latter could be risky if a tenant reneged on the rent, it could be a regular and reliable source of income.

More regularly, goods bought would be recycled, again and again. Lily White describes:

> Tot stalls. That's how they used to clothe the children. All the tot stalls used to do a roaring trade down there [Lambeth Walk]. Everybody used to wear second-hand, third-hand, fourth-hand clothes. Get them on the tot stalls . . .

Furniture, similarly, would be passed down and sold again.

At a more complicated level, this conversion involved the intervention of the pawnbroker. Pawning involved raising cash on the deposit of goods. The pawnbroker charged interest which had to be paid back before the goods could be redeemed. Those who failed to pay back the interest each week forfeited the goods and, in order to redeem the goods, the principal had to be paid back as well. Those goods which had failed to be redeemed were then sold.

Amy Green described one well known pawnbroker's.

Harvey and Thompson's had the pawn part, see, then there was Harvey and Thompson's shop and they sold a lot of second-hand stuff there, you know, the things that were pledged and people wasn't able to get out because they didn't have any money. Bargains they were, when you think of it. Paid 25 bob [£1.25] for my wedding ring in there. Don't think it was very lucky because since then I think it must have been someone who was very sorry to part with it and I think they passed it on to me, you know? My mother-in-law it was, her idea, to go into Harvey and Thompson's and get a second-hand ring. And I bought a ticket off of somebody for that one, down the walk.

As often as not, goods so bought would be entered again by their new purchasers into the credit market. Indeed, the pawnbrokers ran a thriving business.

Kitty Barnet recalled:

When you pawned anything in those days they had a pen what used to write three lots. A pen with three nibs on it, one stick, and it wrote three things and they wrote the three tickets out with that. They used to charge you a halfpenny for the ticket and a halfpenny in a shilling [5p] interest a week. It was slaughter, really . . .

In 1902 the branch of Harvey and Thompson's in the Walworth Road was prosecuted for doing business on Whit Sunday.[2] Their defence was that poor people liked to have their best clothes for the holiday and that there had been so many people trying to redeem their pledges the previous night that they were forced to open on Sunday to serve them all. That Saturday, 2,332 pledges had been redeemed.

Until well into the 1950s a visit to the pawnbroker was a regular weekly event for many working-class families: 'in Monday, out Friday'. It was an essential part of the domestic economy. It wasn't just luxuries that were pawned – often they had long since gone to satisfy the appetite of the Poor Law or the means test, and it was essentials, such as clothing and bedding, that had to be sacrificed.

Tricia Dempsey:

My mum used to do all the washing Monday mornings, get it dry and get them all folded up to go to the pawn shop and she used to say to my sister, 'Don't let them open the middle.' Because the old man's pants had a hole in them!

Food was bought, or the rent paid, through converting personal possessions into cash. Ada Terry:

I used to do me washing. Iron the sheets, make them all nice and square, put them in the pillowcase, put them behind the baby's head in the pram, go to the pawn shop, look round to see if anybody was coming. And that was enough money for me rent . . .

Often the same article would be pawned week after week, and the articles themselves would assume a value as convertible currency. Indeed most items had two values, a use value and a pawn value. Molly Nelson:

When my poor husband was out of work I used to go cleaning doorsteps and that. Or do my landlady's washing. Do a neighbour's, over Lambeth Baths. One of our neighbours says to me, 'Ain't you got no money, Molly?' I used to say 'No'. She said 'Borrow the washing till Friday.' Used to borrow the washing and pawn it.

But one day, my poor husband had a shilling [5p] bet, and he won £20. 'Course, we was moneylenders, wasn't we? He goes to Burton's and buys a suit for £5. Well, I used to borrow that every week, didn't I?

And of the two values, the more important was the pawn value, which had to be maintained above all. Violet Harris:

I remember the time our mum said to me, 'Viley, look after them shoes because you know they've got to go back pawn Monday. And if you muck them up, they won't give you money . . .

With skilful management, a great deal of credit could be

squeezed out of a single item or items, as Violet Harris describes:

> I'd been in there myself, and say 'same as last week'. That would be about three bob [15p], you know. 'No, it's not so good this week. What did you do to it?' 'Oh, go on, I'm going to bring it out Saturday.' So we could tide ourselves over . . .

Mostly it was the women who used the pawnbroker, entering a cycle of credit that could be broken only with difficulty. It often caused domestic violence. Marjorie Rowlands and Violet Neal:

> One day Mum decided she had to pawn her wedding ring. Now, that was a crime. Oh, it was terrible . . . So she buys one out of Woolworth's and gets her own off. My father never knew the ring was in pawn, because I think he would have throttled her. And my sister says to her when she come down one day, 'Mum,' she said, 'I'm going to, for your birthday, I'm going to get your ring out of pawn. Don't you ever let it go in there again.'
>
> So we go up the pawn shop and get the ring out. Well, when we came back, we couldn't get the Woolworth's ring off. Oh, it was a panic. And she was saying 'Your father'll kill me, your father will kill me.' And she had a big red finger, because it was on her paralysed hand, you see. And every time you pulled the finger out [straight], after a while it would take your hand and close up with your hand on it. And do you know how we got it off? We put piles of soap on it and we got an old vice fixed on the back and we pulled, and we finally got it off. But had he've known, he would have gone mad.

Sal Beckford:

> My chap came home one day and he said, I had a stew on, so he said, 'Will it be long, only,' he says, 'I'm going to a meeting.' He hadn't enough stamps on his card to get unemployment money so he had to go to what they call a means test. Anyway, he said, 'Do us a favour, mate, while I'm having me tea, get me trousers out.'

I'd only pawned them, hadn't I? So I goes over to me mother's. I didn't tell, I just walked out over the road. Anyway, a woman in the house right at the top give me a lovely red coat and it had a nice fur on it. She didn't like the colour and she hadn't wore it long so she give it to me, that was me best coat, hanging behind the door in the bedroom. Anyway, I goes over to my mother because I'd pawned his trousers and I didn't want him to know.

When I come back my daughter said to me, 'Daddy ain't half been going off about you.' I said, 'What about?' 'He wants to know where his trousers is.' So I said, 'Oh.' So she said, 'Know what he's done?' I said, 'No, love, what's he done?' 'You know your best coat, what you had?' 'Yeah.' My girl said, she said, 'He's torn it all up!' He'd torn me best coat up, in a temper. When I went in the front room, there it was, ripped in half, all on the floor.

Anyway, when he comes in, I've gone to bed. 'Wake up,' he said, 'you're not asleep. Wake up. Where's me trousers? I suppose they're in the pawn shop. When I walk along there'll be the crease lines.' I said, 'I had a penny to have them hung up so there won't be no lines on them.' I paid a penny to have them hung up.

There were, of course, other ways of obtaining credit in the 1920s and 1930s. Amy Green remembers the salesmen known as the 'weekly men', or the 'tally men'.

They used to come round for firms, furniture firms or drapery firms, get a commission. I suppose it wasn't much wages in those days, you know. Nothing was very much money, but we didn't have very much money to work with. We was hard up, even though the stuff was cheap, we still was finding it a struggle, see, so people who were of good principle were glad of somebody come round, like. There used to be a firm called Twist and I used to have my curtains off of him. 1s.6d. [7½p] a week and they used to have lovely curtains, nice, rings at the bottom, beautiful . . . you didn't have a lot of money but for 1s. 6d. you could have a nice little bill and keep your place nice. Chenille curtains, 25 bob [£1.25] a pair. See, we used to have curtains at our door in those days and things on your mantelpiecing. Horrors! Washing mad I should think – and no washing machine!

Goods bought on credit this way would also have a pawn value. Amy Green comments:

That's really why Harvey and Thompson's thrived, I think. People who was hard up, they couldn't afford the payment but at least they had these parcels. Put them in there for a few bob and then afterwards, after so long, Harvey and Thompson's used to put them in the shop for sale, so they were pretty reasonable to buy.

Another alternative to raising money was through a moneylender, usually a local, whose circumstances were marginally better than the neighbours', but who, unlike the pawnbroker, did not take goods in exchange for cash. Money would only be lent on a good name or reputation. For the moneylender there was no security against defaulters, save finally a resource to the law or, more commonly, a form of moral blackmail. Queenie Thomas describes a woman who:

. . . sold watercress and celery and she was a moneylender too. This would have been in the late 1920s, and people had to deal off her because she lent them money and some of the old rubbish that she used to serve up to them – all stale stuff. I never had no money off her, but I wouldn't have the stuff and she could be quite rude. Very rude she could be.

She sold radishes, salads. It was a large family of them because she'd got another sister further down the road with a stall, and she had another sister. She used to have her daughter serving and all. They used to live down Paradise Street, down the Walk. They were all pretty comfortable. She was the one that used to be a devil, especially if she had a drink. Her husband, because he was only a little bloke, she used to knock him sick. I suppose he just took it. He couldn't hit her. She used to show him up terrible, didn't she?

Molly Nelson says:

When we had the old fires, go and get seven pound coal . . .
couldn't afford a hundredweight, well, you was a moneylender if you could. I used to borrow a pound off the woman
in the Cut. I used to buy loads of lettuces, old rotten stuff,
before she'd lend me the pound.

Kitty Barnet:

. . . she was a moneylender, my mother-in-law. People used
to come and borrow odd money as they called it. Say they
borrowed ten bob [50p], well, the weekend, they'd give her
10s.10d. [54p], like a penny in the shilling. And if they
borrowed a pound, they would give her 20d. [9p]. And if you
couldn't pay the interest, couldn't pay the pound back, you
went on paying the interest.

    She was quite well off compared to some standards. They
even used to pawn their clothes, and sell her the pawn
tickets, and such as sheets and blankets and things. They
couldn't afford to get them out and, say they'd pawned a
thing for a pound, perhaps they'd sell her the ticket for about
ten bob. She'd go and get them out and then she'd flog them
again at more money. Yeh, that was how they used to live.

Attitudes towards the moneylenders reflected conflicting
emotions. Moneylenders were local people, like themselves,
who stood to gain out of the poverty of their neighbours. At the
same time, they represented a crucial fall-back, beyond and
behind the pawnbroker. An unredeemed pledge was property
– and income – lost. But an unpaid debt to a moneylender was
the loss of a good name. Yet the very word 'moneylender' was a
term of abuse – as was the suggestion of being in debt to a local
creditor. (The pawn shop did not count as 'debt'.)

Maintaining a good name was vital for corner shop credit.
Marjorie Rowlands and Viley Neal:

We'd get all our shopping on the Tuesday, and we'd say
'How much is that, Arnold?' He'd say, 'Fifteen shillings

[75p]. Do you want it delivered?' 'Yes, please. And we'll pay you Friday.' We never paid him when we did the shopping. Even if we had it, we would never pay him. We always paid him Friday.

Friday was, of course, pay day.

The other side to the coin of credit was, of course, the thrift club. The tally man's credit was an early form of hire purchase. But many people preferred not to enter into unnecessary debt, and would pay so much a week into a boot club or a clothing club and wait until enough had accumulated before they took possession of the article. Tricia Dempsey:

I didn't have anything much when I left school in 1951. Nobody did and it would take you ages. You'd have a Bradford cheque for about £2s.10s. [£2.50] and you'd pay half a crown [12½p] a week. A Bradford cheque was like, well, I suppose all it was was a credit paper and you could use it in most of the shops in the Walk, the shoe shops, and somebody called once a week and you paid half a crown a week. And when I think of the scrape my mum had paying about 5s. [25p] a week, paying into the Christmas loan club. And Christmas you'd get £13 and she'd have to pay for everything over Christmas. And clothes for the three of us, and all on this £13 . . . That was all before we left school. But she went to the pawn shop, too. Everybody did it. Even my nan used to do it. She'd wash and iron bedlinen, sheets, pillowslips and pawn them for 3s.6d. [17½p], half a crown. Everybody did. This must have been immediately after the war.

Before the Second World War, credit, from the pawn-broker, the tally man, the moneylender or – by delaying the rent – the landlord was a major mechanism for stretching the family budget. For the most part, such credit was small-scale and, on the whole, when it was taken its repayment was carefully accounted for. Although the interest costs were high, it could remain a stable, short-term but regular and easy system of credit, providing that customers did not overreach themselves. If too much was borrowed then, clearly, the dangers of forfeiture were immense. And forfeiture meant not simply the loss of the goods but the loss of any use of those goods to raise loans in the future. But for the most part, those who used the pawnbroker on a regular basis were restricted in their borrowing by the meagreness of their own possessions. The danger came when goods bought on credit elsewhere were then pawned and two credit payments were required to be met out of a single pledge.

Although the pawnbroker and moneylender remained the easiest and most obvious form of credit for ready cash, by the 1930s other forms of credit were becoming more available and more widely used. The growth and development of hire purchase began to offer to many working-class people the possibility of acquiring some of the fruits of prosperity. But hire purchase was restricted to those in regular employment, and thus accentuated the gap between the employed and the unemployed. Terms were easily available, although the fear of repossession was a potent deterrent to missing payments.

Sue Dexter:

We got the furniture and things on hire purchase. I mean, we got a nice home together there and we just finished paying for it when he was called up for the Army. I had a piano as well over there, had a really nice home. And then he got called up for the Army. Well, I remember we had only one payment to pay on the piano and I was so frightened that I wouldn't be able to pay it, I asked them to come and take the piano back. Yeah, it nearly killed me because he used to play the piano quite a bit and I thought, well, it would be nice for the children. And then of course he went into the Army and when he went in I was only getting 32*s*. [£1.60] a week to keep two children and myself and pay the rent and . . . a lot of people got into debt and were evicted. I always made sure I paid me rent.

After the Second World War, and throughout the 1950s and 1960s hire purchase as a form of credit continued to expand nationally. There was a significant expansion of mail order firms offering payment by instalment and, later, credit sales. The credit offered was on the purchase of goods and though repaying the loan including interest clearly cost more than buying with cash, the advantages of weekly terms in fact disguised the high overall cost and, indeed, presented this form of credit almost as a form of saving. Above all, for those in regular employment, this form of credit purchasing provided the means to participate in the advantages of a consumer society.

In recent years the growth of finance houses offering instant 'personal' loans has been remarkable. The interest costs on these loans is high, but for low-paid workers or those on a fluctuating income, they represent one of the few forms of borrowing available. Banks are often reluctant to lend without an assured guarantee of repayment, or collateral.

Short-term borrowing has always been a feature of working-class budgeting. With a small or fluctuating income, both budgeting and saving present problems. Complicated mathematics were, and are, involved, as income is recycled within the street, and within the household.

Marjorie Rowlands and Violet Neal:

We do it now. I mean, I keep her light money, I pay the milkman, I pay the rent, and what I have to pay her, we sort of tally up and tally up and we deduct, and my kids say, 'Mum, how you two ever work yourselves out, I don't know.' But it seems a pattern over the years, don't it? I mean, after I got married and had my children, I used to go and borrow half a crown [12½p] off my mum. Well, I looked after her. She used to say, 'How much have I got to give you?' And I'd say 'Oh, give me a pound, Mum.' But then, in a sense, I got it back another way because she used to buy everything for my two kids . . .

Between the wars, the weekly expenditure for most households could be anticipated on a regular basis. But in the post-war period, the widespread use of utilities such as electricity, gas and telephone has changed the pattern of weekly budgets. Few households now have a coin-slot meter, which made it possible to budget and judge the weekly consumption. Most bills come in quarterly – and always higher than anticipated. This can and does pose problems in payment for some families, when the temptation to take on a personal loan or risk being cut off is at its highest.

But in addition to occasional large bills (and it is possible to arrange for these to be deducted weekly) there are the requirements of everyday living. And then there are purchases which, according to your point of view, may be considered luxuries or necessities.

The dream of the cost-efficient housewife in her labour-saving home, which ran parallel with increased incomes and the fall in real price of consumer durables, led to a decline in public facilities, such as the wash-house. In most post-war council housing design little account was taken of the practicalities of housework. Limited storage space was one problem, at a time when the decline in daily shopping required greater storage facilities. Limited drying space was another. Some of the older tenements have gardens, and most of the housing built between the wars offered some form of communal drying facility. But many post-war flats have neither. Karen Howard:

> I've got a washing machine, but I've got nowhere to dry them. I went into the LEB, I said – I told them the truth – I said 'I'm single. I've got two kids. I get £48 a week coming in.' He said, 'Well, there's no way you can have a tumble drier.' He said 'It's not us, I'd do it, but it's the office . . .' We can't get nowhere. I've tried the Provident. I told them the truth. Someone came round here. He said 'How much do you want to borrow?' I said 'Can I have £150?' That was £6 a week back. Well, that was easy, easy. So he said 'I've put it all in for you.' He rang me up this morning and he said, 'I'm

sorry, love,' he said, 'It's not down to us, it's the office itself, they won't do it.'

Because I'm a single parent. You see, I want some action done. I want someone to sort of help us whether we can get HP, things like that. But we can't, can't get nothing. The only thing we can, if we get two guarantors. But what's the difference? If you're married, you don't have to have a guarantor . . .

As has always been the case, those with the most vulnerable incomes have least access to credit. Many women, single parents on social security, have almost all credit avenues closed to them. Banks, credit sales, hire purchase and finance houses remain closed shops as far as they are concerned. They are forced to borrow from the traditional source, the pawnbroker, at interest rates of 24 per cent[3], but with no questions asked. (Yet, ironically, those rates compare quite favourably with much 'in house' credit. A Marks and Spencer Charge-card, for instance, offers an interest rate of 26.8 per cent.)

But pawnbroking, too, has changed. Reflecting the relative affluence of the 'new' working class, the small weekly pledges – never that economical – have been replaced with high-value goods, such as jewellery, watches, cameras and high-price electrical items. Also, pawnbroking has ceased to be a local facility.

The Lambeth Walk branch of Harvey and Thompson's is a case in point. Once the linchpin of the local sub-economy, it combined jewellery retail with pawnbroking. After the re-development of Lambeth Walk in the mid 1970s, 'Harvey's' moved to new premises in the shopping precinct, still combining retail with broking. But by 1981 the combined effects of the slump and the opening of many cut-price jewellery shops made retailing more difficult and the company closed down its retail outlets and put all its energy into pawnbroking. At the same time, it transferred its premises from Lambeth Walk to Lower Marsh – in the hope of broadening its trade to include office workers and commuters in the Waterloo area.[4]

Pawnbroking has now become a highly profitable business again, but it has also changed its image. Discreet in its smoked glass splendour, the pawnbroker hopes to compete, in respectability, with the building society and the bank. It aims, therefore, to attract a wider clientele, to lose its reputation as the 'poor man's banker'. But in the process, the local relationship between broker and client has changed, as has the nature of the goods they are prepared to accept. Harvey and Thompson's now will only deal in jewellery pledges, on the grounds that they are easier to handle, and 'space means money'.

Karen Howard:

It's all gold, gold and diamonds. There's Harry, used to be down Lambeth Walk. He's a good old stick, he was. He never used to take watches. They stopped doing watches about two years ago. But he still takes them – used to take my mum's in. He's known her for years. Used to go down to him and say, 'Harry, how much can I have on that?' He used to look at it, you see, 'Give us it here.' So, see now, they've got a thing about weighing. But he didn't, used to cheat a little bit. He'd say 'here, couple extra . . .'

A gate bracelet he give you about £40, £45. But it's always a three-month ticket now. It's all right getting them in, getting the money – not too good getting them out. I've lost two bracelets over that. They put them in the auction, then they sell them. They're right cheats, you know. They sell them for more money than what you pawned them for. I pawned a bracelet for £40 and I didn't get it out and about six months later. 'Sorry, we've sold it.' And you know, I bet they sold it for about £80.

It's me mum does it now. She takes all hers and if I want one taken, she'll take it. Well, might as well, I've got one left. Down the pawn shop. Well, can't be proud in this world can you, mate, nowadays?

Pawnbrokers now come under the Consumer Credit Act, but for their working-class clients this means little. Between the wars, small amounts could be redeemed feasibly within the weekly budget. Now jewellery yields higher profits, but the redemption costs are high – too high to be easily fitted within the budget. It is no longer a weekly loan process, but rather the resort of the desperate, so the chances of redemption are even more reduced.

Deirdre Patel:

> People still do it, you know, a lot of people. I know a lot of people that have done it, they've really been down, you know? I do sometimes . . . I only got about £8 on one time, but I was desperate, really was. Just left it in and that was it.

The other side to raising cash, is spending it. Lambeth Walk before the Second World War was, as Amy Green recalls:

> . . . a big market, like East Lane. But it wasn't chartered, like East Lane was chartered, though this was the oldest market. That's why they've been able to ruin it. It was Lambeth Borough Council that more or less helped ruin the Walk. They never wanted the market. When we were down there they used to say they couldn't afford the market, they couldn't afford the cleaning of it, you see? Used to cost so much money to be cleaned up. They always said that, made all complaints about the market and that. Then it was somebody had a grandiose scheme, at the GLC it was, to build a precinct, and most of this area is all tinned up like that.
>
> And we had big shops down there, we had nice shops down there. We had a Peacries, where they used to have like an in and out shop, where you could go in and come right round. Sold everything. Curtaining, sheets and things and frocks and, well, like a proper draper, drapery outfitters. Before that, there was a big shop and they sold prams and furniture. Stones, that was. Big shop, and if you took your pram there, they'd mend it for you. It doesn't seem possible, to see that Walk as it was to as it is now – to think there was so much, so many places in it, and it was so busy. Now, it looks dead.

. . . then there was a wallpaper shop . . . all along there, if you went down Lambeth Walk you was sure you could buy more or less what you were looking for. Anything. There was a wool shop, and there was a fish shop, a wet fish shop and a fried fish shop. Lovely fried fish. That was all that side, and all the way along, there was a variety of shops, right?

There was a good butcher's down the Walk, very good butchers. Coppins, that was another shop. It was a beautiful shopping area. When we were down there, first down there, it was thriving. 1928, that's when the shops were all good shops. It was a nice friendly atmosphere and people all knew each other. Pubs used to do all right because it wasn't expensive like to go into a pub. And that was where people used to go, didn't spend much money. Like we used to go in a pub, used to be a night out, used to have people, like entertainers, and things like that, local people that could sing . . .

Doesn't seem possible, if you look at that area down there, it doesn't look as though all those shops could be down there. But of course, Lambeth Walk went right to the top – the top end there used to be people with second-hand stalls, up that end, by the baths. Lot of people used to buy second-hand stuff. Tot stalls. And people used to get a good living out of that because you could buy little children's clothes, see. Those days, just for tuppence or whatever it was, they could get themselves some nice bits and pieces . . .

What I'm trying to get over is the fact that Lambeth Walk – you were able to go anywhere in Lambeth Walk for what you wanted, whatever you thought of, even on a Sunday morning. And there were several good chemists. There was a lovely chemist, Douglas, you could go there with all your ailments, and your animals as well. He'd treat you. He was ever such a lovely man, him and his sister. And he sold his own potions as well, Douglas's ointment.

In 1938, there were 159 retail shops in Lambeth Walk, excluding the market stalls. But Lambeth Walk was by no means the only shopping area. The Cut, Lower Marsh, Vauxhall Street, China Walk, Tyer's Street – all were thriving shopping thoroughfares, supplemented by many individual shops interspersed throughout the neighbourhood. In addition to the shops, Lambeth Walk, the Cut and Lower Marsh all supported lively markets. And there were, as well, the barrow boys and the itinerant traders.

Gracie Tarbuck:

The rag and bone man, with the bell. 'Any old iron! Any old lamps!' he used to shout. And the old vinegar barrow used to come round with the block salt. And the hearth stone. 'Vinegar and hearthstone and salt' Great rocks of salt!' We used to hearthstone our doorsteps. Who hearthstones their doorsteps today? I ask you!

And the old cockles used to come round and the shrimps and winkles used to come round. They were cheap, weren't they? About tuppence a pint. Cockles. That used to be your regular Sunday tea. Shrimps or cockles. The old cow heel man used to come round with the tripe. He used to sell cow heels, all cooked, all jelly, didn't he? Used to come round the pubs with it, with a big basket with a cloth in and they'd have a vinegar bottle and their paper and you'd buy half a cow heel. Might be tuppence, might be thruppence. Just a titbit, a titbit.

Then there used to be the old mint lady, she'd sell ha'pence of mint and ha'pence of sage in her basket. And parsley, mint, sage and parsley, in a basket. Horseradish. Ordinary woman, she used to be there all the time. Used to sell horseradish what you grate yourself. And the old laven-der woman used to come round singing 'so many sticks a penny', the old lavender people. You'd get the old muffin man, he'd come down the road. 'Muffins and crumpets!' Chopped bundles of wood, they used to come round selling that. They used to do that round the Walk, and he used to chop the wood up there and tie it in bundles.

There was the cat's meat man, Mr Mallet, in Ethelred

Street. He used to come round with meat on a stick. And all the cats used to follow him, and the dogs and all. They had one in the Cut, too, and Black Prince Road. He'd come round with his basket with his cat's meat. The one in Ethelred Street was a beautiful clean shop, but they used to go round with a basket on their arm, with all this meat on skewers. Meat kettle on the top. Ha'porth of meat, the old cats running round, cats and dogs, following this man. I think he give as much away as he sold sometimes. Good-natured people . . .

In addition there was a plentiful supply of shops which sold ready cooked food. Gracie Tarbuck:

There was one thing the men used to like – the old sheep's head. We used to go down the tripe shop and they used to cook the sheep's head and they were lovely. And jellied eels and stewed eels.

Violet Harris:

. . . George's pudding shop, top of the Cut. It was known all over England. Lovely plum puddings. Baked potatoes, cheap. A full size plate. They'd make a plum pudding, cut it in four, ha'penny each piece. And the baked potatoes, put some stuffing on . . . Didn't know what we were eating. Could have been cockroaches for all we knew. George's pudding shop. Everyone in London knew that. And the funny part about it, you know, when you look down the area there was the kitchen and we used to lay down there and look and all you could see was rats. Rats running, big as cats, all round the pipes. Literally running alive with rats. It was smashing grub, though. A baked potato, shove that stuffing in, blooming great spoonful of stuffing. You'd turn your nose up at it now.

And the pork butcher's at the top of the Walk, German pork butcher's. They used to cook their pork. Saveloys, pease pudding, faggots. It was a German, they mobbed him up over the war. You could go in there and buy faggot and pease pudding. Ha'penny faggot and ha'porth of pease pudding and you had it in a newspaper. Walk along with your sav in your hand, stick it in the pease pudding . . . And fish and chips. Ha'porth of fish, ha'porth of taters. Half-penny and ha'porth . . .

Tricia Dempsey:

Even after World War 2 Lambeth Walk had every shop imaginable. My favourite being the pie and mash shop. School holidays meant pie and mash every day. It only cost 8*d.* [3½p] and I loved it. Still do. Can't change old habits!

The number and variety of shops reflected the lives and the needs of the local community. For working-class people in the inner city, shopping, between the wars, was local. No one in this area of Lambeth had a car, and a bus ride added cost to the food bill. Shopping was often done daily, for cramped housing meant little room for long-term storage of food, and with no refrigerators, fresh food could not be kept for very long, particularly in the summer months.

Budgeting as well was done, often, on a daily basis. Casual workers would be paid on a daily rate, and even for those in regular employment, there was rarely sufficient slack to shop in advance for a week. Far greater control over the budget could be exercised if the money was parcelled out daily, even though shopping that way was less economical. Indeed, economies of scale were – and are – only possible when there is surplus cash initially.

The amounts bought were invariably small, sufficient for the day's needs and no more. For the shopkeeper, survival also meant flexibility, especially when the demand was for small amounts, at the cheapest possible cost. Violet Harris:

We couldn't afford 7 pounds of coal, like, so mother broke up a chair so we could have a warm, have a bit of warm when Dad came home. She couldn't afford a penny for the gas. Never had no bacon or nothing. Of course, mother could only have a quarter of coal when she had, like, a bit extra money. Wasn't very often. She didn't often have a penny to put in the gas so we often had to rely on the old fire, with a piece of wood. On the fire there was an oven, you know, at the side. She could make a nice cake but only with a bit of flour, half and half water and milk and a few currants. Used to be beautiful. But of course we used to think ourselves very lucky if we went home and found a bit of cake on the rack, you know. But other than that . . . batter puddings and that, but that was when she could afford an egg and skimmed milk off the man that used to come round the streets selling it, see. I don't think he had the full, just the skim milk, see. Friday's dinner was rice boiled with water. That was what filled you up. Of course, then it was only about a penny a pound and you could get a pennorth of jam from the grocer's shop, bit of treacle . . .

. . . Ha'porth of jam, a penny packet of tea, pennorth of mustard pickles, in a cup, farthing for the milk, pennorth of jam on a plate . . .

Shops kept late hours – many men were not paid till late on a Friday or a Saturday night, and it was only then that the food shopping for the weekend could be done. The art of shopping involved getting not only the place, but also the time, right. Food shops also had no refrigeration, and so meat, for instance, was best bought late on a Saturday night when the butcher's stock would have to be sold off. Marjorie Rowlands and Viley Neal remember:

You used to go down there on a Saturday evening up to nine o'clock and have a penny piece of Tottenham – that's a cake with pink icing on the top. Lovely it was. A pennorth of Tottenham, then they used to get the joints cheaper. That was why it was always packed Saturday evenings because they got the meat cheaper. They'd auctioneer them in the end. You know what's killed all that? The bloody freezers, that's what's done all that. All this prepacked food, dehydrated and all. I mean, you can't go in the shop now and take a jug with you for milk, or pickles . . .

And Carrie Telford:

> The Cut's still there, but it's nothing to what it was. You know the Lower Marsh, well that used to be two sides of the street, chock-a-block and if you went along there Saturday nights, ten, wasn't it? Ten o'clock, auctioneering the meat off and that, get rid of it because they didn't have fridges to keep it in, see. They used to knock the meat out then. We used to wait, and we used to get a whole joint of lamb for 1s.6d. [7½p]. And the fishmongers was the same . . .

Many greengrocers would sell cheaply their 'speck' fruit and vegetables – that produce which had been damaged, or was simply unfresh – a bargain to be had usually towards the end of the day. Violet Harris:

> 'A pennorth of specks, please,' She used to go down there, 'a pennorth of specks, please'. One of these scoop brass scales, you know, full of oranges, apples, pears, whatever was in season. They was just touched on the top. They wouldn't sell them, they were very fussy you know what they sold then, and my dad used to be about an hour doing them taking them all out, all the bits of soft stuff on the oranges, and, course, we had a bit of fruit each day for a penny, see?

The cooked food shops sold their leftovers. Marjorie Rowlands and Viley Neal:

> . . . a lot of families would go over the fish shop and ask for two pennorth of cold fish, and you'd get quite a bit. Well, that was a meal. And our mother used to go into the pie shop and get a jug of liquor, so you had cold fish hotted up, mashed potato, and eel liquor over. We used to think it was lovely, but fancy eating it today!

Bakers sold their stale bread cheap . . . such bargains were vital to the survival of many families. Gladys Harman:

When we was kids we used to go and take a pillowcase with you and we'd buy three pennorth of stale bread, loaves and rolls. By the time we had got home we'd ate half the rolls and you went the next day round different butchers and you bought three pennorth of giblets. Bag full for thruppence. Stale cakes. You could get about ten of them for a ha'penny. You went in the fish shop in the morning and you bought two pennorth of cold fish and you'd get about six or seven pieces of fish that was cooked the night before. We used to buy what we call a farthing's worth of cracklings. As you were frying fish there's all bits of batter comes off. They call them cracklings and they'd give you a paperful that big for a farthing. Bacon bones. Sometimes we got little bits of bacon in it. You'd cut it up so you could make a bacon pudding, bacon and onion pudding. My mother used to put all the bacon in the frying pan and get them all fried up and leave all the gravy, you know, all the bacon fat and then she used to fry our stale bread in the bacon fat so that we all had a lump of stale bread with bacon.

Between the wars shopping was well adapted to the needs of local people. The major reconstruction of the area following the Second World War began to alter this easy fit. Marjorie Rowlands and Viley Neal:

I think we're the forgotten city round here . . . I mean, we got no shopping facilities round here. We got Tesco's, but I mean, we had every shop you wanted in St George's Road . . . Ain't got nothing now. It's all gone.

Although the shopping precinct at the Elephant and Castle has long since been finished, many of the shop premises remain unlet. There is a Woolworth's, and a large Tesco's, a couple of butcher's, a baker's, two chemist's (including a branch of Boots), a greengrocer's. There is a Wimpy and a Golden Egg. There is a W. H. Smith, an Aquazoo, a shoe repairer's, a shoe shop, a DIY shop. There are boutiques, jeweller's, and hairdresser's. There is a shop that sells a miscellaneous assortment of cheap goods. There are an electrical shop, a gift shop, a travel agent's, a branch of a building society, a bank, and there is a large Home Pride furniture store. In theory this precinct satisfies consumer needs. It is possible to buy most of the commodities required for daily living. In practice, each shop has a virtual monopoly and, apart from the supermarket, they all sell at relatively high prices.

The shopping precinct is approached through underground subways. Smelling of urine, they give shelter to the local alcoholics and junkies. Their bleak, tiled walls offer unlimited space for local graffiti, colourful but angry. They are not pleasant places to walk through, but threatening tunnels of potential violence and viciousness. Badly lit, and often empty, they are the gauntlet that must be run before the shopping can be done.

In Lambeth Walk the market no longer exists. Carol Phillips:

> That's awful. I mean, there's the Lambeth Walk but since they made it into a pedestrian shopping centre, it's awful, it's really dreadful. Before they pulled all the old shops down there used to be all the stalls, there used to be a Sainsbury's down there, but if you go down there you can't buy anything down there, like . . . there isn't anything at all, and if you go into the Co-op they haven't hardly got anything. It's really gone down. You ask anybody, and they always say it has really gone down. It's dreadful.

There is now a mega-Sainsbury's in Vauxhall, designed for the car-owner and catering keenly for the middle classes who have moved into Clapham and Kennington. One or two corner shops survive. But the markets of the Cut and Lower Marsh are shadows of their former selves, catering for the office workers from County Hall or the Shell Centre, and now dependent on them.

Judy Chalmers runs a market stall in Lower Marsh:

I only sort of like always refer to them two because they're the sort of people, if they come to your stall, you know them because they've got their badges on. There's probably a lot more government buildings round here, like Education, Central Office of Information, Hercules Road, but it's definitely the office workers that's keeping them. I hate to say it because I think they've already got the idea, you know, if they was to leave the area we would die . . . [but] they're taking up ground that could be houses anyway, really, so it wouldn't follow on. But I hate to say that they're keeping the stalls going anyway, put it that way.

The shopping precincts are now as if caught in a time warp. Their construction presupposed an age of continuing affluence. The local economic and demographic changes, as well as national economic recession, has meant that North Lambeth is one of the least affluent areas not only of London, but nationally. Moreover, the assumption of easy mobility underlying ever bigger supermarkets was never relevant for women in this area. It always presupposed that women had access to a car, or at least adequate public transport. Few families have cars. In 1981, in Lambeth as a whole, 71 per cent of council tenants did not have access to a car.[5] On the Kennington Park Estate 81 per cent did not have a car, and on the Tanswell Estate, 80 per cent did not.[6]

Without a car, shopping with children in a pram, buggy or simply in tow needs to be local. Local shops, as always, are expensive. It is cheaper to buy in a supermarket, but the supermarket is a bus ride away. It is therefore more economical to buy more on a single shopping expedition. But that means more to carry, which, with children, is often a physical impossibility. More trips are required, more bus rides, more hassle . . . more strain on the weekly budget, more strain on the daily nerves.

Jackie Davy has two children and works as a childminder. In addition,

I work Saturdays, so I can't do my shopping Saturdays. It's not a free day for me. Sundays the shops are shut. So normally I take Stephen to school in the morning, which means I pop in that corner shop for the immediate needs, which is an expensive way of doing shopping. But he's not been at school for the last fortnight, because the lady's off, [so] I've done practically no shopping. I've been popping into the shop and dragging them all with me. [But] you can't carry more than your immediate needs anyway. Pete has to get the potatoes for me on Saturday because I can't carry potatoes up as well as everything else I have to carry.

As in this case, some husbands do help out at the weekend, or with late-night shopping at Sainsbury's. And shopping becomes less of a problem as children grow older. But for the most part, the requirements of working-class women are the traditional ones: local shops at competitive prices. And these requirements are not met.

The commercial move towards supermarkets and the economic and demographic changes which have altered the provision of local supply is one of the major causes of discontent in North Lambeth. It affects not just the mother with young children, but women of all ages for whom shopping – always a delicate balance of income and expenditure – is a major feature of daily life. The nearest, substantial, traditional market is 'the Lane', East Street, in Walworth, but that always means a bus ride. The lack of facilities is a visible outward sign of the internal economic warping of the area.

The commercial decline has had both economic and cultural effects. Those local shops that survive maintain some relationship with the community. However, the corner shops are limited in number and the store life of the food they sell is also limited. When shopping was done locally the turnover was high, and, as a result, a variety of shops selling a variety of goods could survive. But a single local corner shop with high prices faces different problems of survival.

The supermarket makes no pretence at a personal relationship between shop and community. What it stocks is the result of market research and marketing, a balance between central supply and availability, and the assessment of the local manager of what will sell. In any case, the catchment represents a far wider constituency than the immediately surrounding area. Though in theory a greater variety of food is available, in practice, purchasing is done on the basis of what is familiar, and, of course, what can be bought from the family's budget. Maggie Thorpe says:

> Half the time I don't know what to get. Beefburgers, fish cakes, cod steaks, soup. Summer's all right, it's easy, innit? Salad. I'm a salad fanatic. I like my salad. But, mostly, I don't know. Like on Mondays we had chops. Now my husband won't eat chops and he won't eat chicken, so I has to buy him, like, sausages. Then Tuesday we had shepherd's pie. That was nice. Then we had pies and corned beef, and today we had egg and chips. But I don't know what to get everybody, do you know what I mean? Like the kids say, 'Oh we'll have fish fingers', and I'll say, 'But Daddy don't like fish fingers', and then he doesn't like fish fingers unless he's got beans. He's a beans fanatic. But I get the same old thing, week after. It drives me coco, you don't know what to buy . . .

With a limited budget there is little attempt to try anything different unless it is pushed by strong advertising. There is nothing new in this. Just that the basic ingredients are more expensive, and now come prepackaged. There is no wet fish shop any more: cod steaks have to suffice. If the shopping is done in a supermarket it makes sense – and this is the intent of the supermarket – to buy meat there. Beefburgers are cheaper, and easier, than buying fresh mince. And if you are buying frozen fish, the frozen burgers are on the same frozen shelf . . . the 'convenience' of the supermarket is designed to reflect the convenience of the food industry.

The convenience food and fast food industries have filled

the hole created by the demise of the local traditional cooked food retailers, the eel and pie shop, or the fish and chip shop. For convenience foods have always been a feature of working-class diet. They provided easy meals, and a break from the daily routine of cooking – in fact, the poor person's restaurant.

Between the wars, and in the immediate post-war period, the facilities in the neighbourhood, from the market to the pawn shop, rested in an intricate economic niche. Goods could be bought locally with money generated locally. Work, income and shopping were closely related. It was possible to survive within the neighbourhood. Now those who live within that neighbourhood compete with those who only work there. Needs, and incomes, differ.

References
1. Maud Pember Reeves, *Round About a Pound a Week*.
2. A version of this, co-written with Ruth Richardson, was published as 'Victorian Pawnography' in *The New Statesman*, 27 May 1983.
3. 1985 rates. Interview with Mr Watson of Harvey and Thompson's, 1985.
4. Ibid.
5. London Borough of Lambeth, *Estate Profiles: 1981 Census Results*.
6. Ibid.

Families

The families which Maud Pember Reeves met were, by her standards, 'respectable'. The mothers were married women and efficient housekeepers. Families have changed, and many aspects of the criterion of 'respectability' which used to differentiate the members of the working class no longer apply. Indeed, perhaps the only constant is the need for dexterity in household management, to make the most out of limited and limiting circumstances, to provide for the children. Maybe this is what 'respectable' is supposed to mean.

Who are the representative families now? And how do they manage on present incomes?

Greta Lynes was born in Jamaica in 1948 and came to England with her parents when she was nine. She now lives in one of the flats built in the 1930s on the China Walk Estate. She was the eldest of eight children.

> Big sister I had to be, you know? I used to hate it. I never even used to get time for my own homework until more or less them lot were in bed. I used to get up in the morning and make breakfast for everyone, get the place organised, wash everybody, get those who had got to be got dressed, before I went to school. Come home from school and do the same thing. Mum had a part-time job in the evening, in between times, when she was pregnant as well. I used to always wonder why Mum used to sleep so much, you know, until I got a bit older! We lived first in Ladbroke Grove, Cambridge Gardens, then I came to Lambeth in 1975.
>
> I was working in the west end, for a market research company, and I decided to have a change. I was going out

with a boy that live round this side, so I just moved one day, just came straight from work, and that was it. The boy I was going with at the time, he was in a council flat, and I just moved in with him. People might say I cheat, but I wouldn't say so. I was twenty-five.

I had moved out of home when I was eighteen. I am a nurse, really, so I had to go in hospital – you start your training at eighteen. I gave up nursing in 1975. I wanted a break from it. I was still doing part-time, weekends, just to get a little extra money again, because I was doing a course that I desperately wanted to do, a computer course, and I needed the money to pay for that. I was fascinated with the computer, and the firm decided they were going to send me on a course. But I'd still be waiting, so I took myself off, I decided to do it privately myself. The firm I was with, they'd always say there were going to do things and they never really got round to it. I don't know if I should say this, it might not go down very well. It was a Jewish company. It makes a lot of difference. I was put down a lot in that company and I didn't like it at all. I was very unhappy – in the end I had to leave. I worked with them for five years . . .

We went out for about a year before I moved round to this side and we never got married, no, because he was from Nigeria, you see, and the culture is a lot different to our culture. It's a very hard culture to get used to. You've got to exercise a lot of tolerance and patience, otherwise you go crazy. It's so strict, you know. He could almost be frightening at times, but I was so keen that I decided that I'd go to evening classes and learn the language, so I did. I picked up a lot from talking and that – I used to write little things down in my notebook. I could understand what they were saying . . . We've been broke up about six, seven years now so I don't have anything to do with it, but I still remember it.

It used to please him ever so much you know, the fact that I took the interest to go and learn it, and I used to do all the cooking . . . we were so close when we were alone [but] when you're out, they're so, they hide all . . . their inhibitions.

They're not allowed to hold hands, they can't cuddle . . . when you're alone its a different thing the love – outside, all this love is hidden and I think it's so wrong – if you've got loving, you let people see it, you know? It helps people to understand you as well. You're coming over natural . . .

I kept saying I didn't think I'm going to like this, him being a Moslem. There's a lot of things that he will do in this country, but the minute he gets home, coming from a very strict Moslem family, he has to stop and I didn't think I could cope with all that – that's one of the reasons I broke up the relationship. All my things were shipped over there, everything I possessed. I was going to go and live there, because that's my first girl's father, you see, get married over there and everything. But then I thought, no. I just decided that's going to be a change of my life, 1979.

I was very lucky. I had to move because the council had to re-modernise the flat. I got this flat then. I've got a very good housing officer and I said to them, 'No way am I going to come out of something into something worse.' Everybody wants to better themselves and I intend to do that with myself.

It was the very day I got that flat I met my husband now. I came and had a look at it and I thought, oh brilliant. On my way back I stopped. The council's doing these flats and I said, 'Do you know anyone that does decorating?' He said 'Yes, but it will be expensive.' And I said, 'Well, I'm sorry, better forget it . . .' So he said, 'Where do you live?' So, you know, telling him where I live. Of course, he came round and had a look at it. He was ever so nice, you know, very shy. And he kept coming every day. He put all the papers up, and helped to paint. He didn't ask me to pay him any money, and I thought, funny . . . Then he just said that he'd like to take me out and it just started from there. Just like that.

We got married in September 1981, before this bundle came along. I was pregnant. I tend to get very large very quickly. I was really huge. I looked as though I was having triplets . . .

My husband's a plasterer, but he lost his job. Got redundant two weeks before my youngest was due and I – because of that, I had her a week early. Brought the labour on.

This unemployment, it's creating an awful lot of problems, you know? Really. He enjoys his job, he loves his job very much and this has made him very depressed, very bitter and – just changed him. Totally different person.

I wish it never really happened to us because we have a lot going for us and it's taken all that away and, you know, it's made things very bitter in lots of little ways, you know? You get Christmas coming and the children, they don't understand that you haven't got the money to buy them Christmas presents, because you don't get allocated money for things like that, and yet they still have to get Christmas presents. It means either you go without something to wear or you go without certain food or a bill has to go unpaid, you know? We were always taught in the West Indies that England is a place paved with gold . . . and there are still some people that think like that and if you tell them they don't believe you because they've never heard of it.

Because of the unemployment, my husband's taken it really bad, you know? Terrible. And we've split up . . . for the time being. I don't know. He's just . . . I went away after, with the children, because he was, you know, behaving very strange and I get a bit upset about it . . . I mean, it's affecting the children . . . he's really taken it bad. It's been about three weeks. He phone, when I got back, to say, you know, that he, he was all right. Don't know where he is, but he was all right. I mean, the unemployment makes men do some really strange things. But the children, every minute, 'Where's my Daddy?' The little one. And the big one. It's affected her at school.

I've been trying to get Liza into a nursery so I could try and go out to work. But that's the thing, you see? When you're married you get nothing, because most of the things are for single parents . . . I'm under a lot of strain and pressure . . . There's so much to cope with over the children. It's all right if you're on your own with children, you're just used to being on your own, so it doesn't make things any more difficult. But when you're used to having a companion, and then find he's gone . . . coming in, knowing that he's not going to come in. It really hurts, you know, it really, really hurts.

I've got a lot of things inside I'd like for my children but because my husband's not working, I'm not working, it makes it very difficult. If I wasn't married, I think I'd be able to move round easier, and I wouldn't have all this worry about my children not getting what I really would like them to have. I mean, I've only got two. They're suffering. Not that my mother had a lot to give me, there were so many of us, but we never went without. And you know, although love shows inside of all this, you've still got to be able to, no matter how depressed you, to exercise the love so the children can see it. I think life as a married mother is very hard, because you do not get anything. I was better off when I was single with my child than now I'm married with my two children.

I don't know where he's living now. I wish I knew. At night now, Liza wants to come into my bed. And I say no. Because the space is for him and I think one day he might think of us, and come back . . .

Greta's experience was raw and painful, made more so by their joint involvement in community groups and the mothers' and toddlers' club, so that at every stage Greta had to explain, or lie, about her husband's absence. Not knowing whether his leaving was to be permanent, not knowing even his where-abouts, had practical implications as well as emotional ones, for it was proving difficult for her to claim extra benefits, and to budget accordingly. But her family, and her husband's family, were supportive, as were her circle of close friends, although many of them had little to spare, and many were still sending money 'back home'.

Her husband's unemployment benefit was £52, but:

That's not what you get – we get £48 a week, and you get it fortnightly (1984). Get taxed as well. They also take out housing benefit and if you want your electricity and gas. By the time it gets to you, you get virtually nothing. If you've got bills, like furniture, paying on things like that, by the time you do all that the money is finished before the fortnight.

Her neighbour, a Mr Sealy, was also unemployed, and had been so for a while. In his fifties, the chances of his finding employment were slim. His wife, Mary, worked as a kitchen assistant for which she received, in 1987, approximately £100 a week. They, too, were Jamaican and had come to Britain as young people in the 1950s, settling finally in North Lambeth. Mary was attending literacy classes at her local adult education centre.

The Sealys had five children, the youngest of whom was under sixteen. None of the older children lived at home or contributed to the family income. The family allowance for the youngest child was £7.25 and other benefits amounted to an additional £32. The income, therefore, for a household of three, was £139.25. They lived in a two-bedroomed council flat and out of their income, spent:

Rent, rates and water	£42.43
Electricity	£6.40 (£75.99 per quarter, higher in winter)
Telephone	£4.16 (£50 per quarter)
Bus fares	£4.50
Personal items	£0.38
School dinners	£5.00
Adult education	£1.00
Entertainment (bingo)	£6.00
Cigarettes	£3.00
Food	£46.52
Total	£119.39
Surplus	£19.86

No insurance was paid, no savings were made and the family owed nothing on HP. Out of the £19.86 per week, money had to be found for clothing, for sending home to Jamaica, for contingencies, such as the television licence, and household cleaning materials (bought in bulk). But a single pair of shoes could remove the surplus one week. On such a tight budget, Mary would, for instance, save the remnants of toilet soap and use it for washing her underwear.

Cost was crucial and she knew, down to the last penny, how much each item cost and how long it could be expected to last. She cooked West Indian food and did her shopping mainly in the market at Brixton and in the large Tesco supermarket there, where the costs were considerably cheaper than in local shops, even though it required a bus ride. She shopped once a week. Her food budget consisted of:

Bread (four loaves)	£1.72 (43p at Tesco; 50p at the corner shop)
Tea	£0.63
Coffee	£2.50
Sugar	£0.88
Milk	£7.00
Soft drinks/beer	£4.26
Peanut butter	£0.48
Butter	£0.50
Margarine	£2.20
Fresh meat	£4.00
Bacon	£1.20
Sausages	£2.00
Cooked meats	£1.40
Fish (fresh)	£3.60
Vegetables	£6.00
Fruit	£2.50
Cheese	£0.86
Spices, etc.	£0.75
Eggs	£1.60

Rice	£1.00
Flour	£1.44
Total	£46.52

Rice was bought in bulk, £30 for 100 lb. delivered, though she had just found another supplier who would deliver for £28. All cake- and biscuit-baking was done by her, and no frozen or ready-made meals were bought. Their diet was varied and Mary Sealy enjoyed cooking and was clearly good at it. Fish featured strongly in their diet. Their meals included ackee, saltfish and rice, rice and peas with chicken in a casserole, roast breadfruit and fresh fish. Sunday breakfast (a special treat) included fried plantain, egg and bacon, black coffee. At about £15.50 per head a week, or £2.20 a day, food accounted for just over one-third of their outgoings; rent amounted to slightly under one-third. They were able to live just within the margins of their income.

Karen West, in 1983, was twenty-one and lived in Vauxhall in one of the older council flats which was due for renovation. It had three rooms. She was a single parent with two pre-school children. She had married at seventeen, and her older child, a girl, was born shortly after. Karen had been born in St Thomas's Hospital and lived in Vauxhall all her life. Her parents were now both out of work, and her father, a porter, had been unemployed for many years. She had been sent to a 'boarding school' (Pottersbury Lodge, Northamptonshire) when she was eight 'because I was a very nervous person and I wouldn't settle down in school. This was from St Thomas's [hospital] that I went.' At sixteen she had left and,

> ... had one or two jobs. I worked in Lipton's, round the corner, for a while and then I was a cleaner in the evenings in the NAAFI and then I couldn't find a job and then I got pregnant with her, and then I got married.
> I first got married in a registry office and had a big reception in my mum's, and that was big! I don't know [how

many], can't count, because the blokes there my dad knows in the pub and that, all his mates, they knew me, so when he went down the pub they all come back with him with crates of beer and all that. We had quite a houseful. Couldn't move! They moved most of their stuff out, and I was out there with her, and I had to hold the plates up high with all the sandwiches on. I couldn't move! I had her, and then I had another, a little boy. But that marriage never really worked out . . .

I'm divorced now. But I'm getting married again. Well, we was planning to get married this month but we got to put it off till June because it's too much having two parties in one month. It was my boy-friend's birthday yesterday so we're having a big party on Saturday. How did I meet him? I used to go out on a Friday night . . . with a mate who lives round the corner and we used to go to a little bingo on a Friday night. Her husband's a chauffeur and this is how I met my bloke. We used to go to the pub for a drink after and my mate's husband told him to come down to the pub one day – and from then on it worked out from there. That was in October and he done my flat right out for me, bought me a little record player, that was for my birthday last year, and now he's bought me a music centre. I already had a video but I didn't have a telly so he bought me that and then we had to have another telly because that went wrong and now we've got two tellies and the kids have got everything now they need and that.

I used to have a big struggle with money. I could never handle money but now I can have money in my purse all week. Whatever I need I just go out and get. He's good too. Like Sunday night we had a party underneath us. My boy-friend slept right through it and I was awake most of the night and in the morning he knew it. He got up, give them their breakfast, bathed them and then he woke me up after and that. He helps a lot. Cooks the dinner on Sunday or if I'm ill he'll see to the kids and cook the dinner and that. They don't see their dad any more. He hasn't got custody or access to them. I don't see him about so they don't think about him or anything, or ask about him. She used to see photos of her first dad and she used to say, 'That's my daddy.' Well, we was over at their great-aunt's, which is my ex-husband's aunt, I'm still friendly with them and they brought some photographs and one was of their own dad and she said, 'I don't know who that is.' She used to say who it was, but now she doesn't bother. They treat the other one as their own dad now.

My boy-friend's got his own business with his mate, like. They do removals and clear-outs and all things like that. He's not really earning much at the moment because it's his mate's own business and he's in a bit of a debt at the moment, so he has to keep their money low. He gets about £60 or £70 a week that's his but it should really be a £100. So, what I do at the moment, I get my family allowance monthly and sometimes when that's due our telephone bill's due so we keep the family allowance for that. But the money I get every week off my other book, that helps out at the moment. But once we've made the marriage arrangements and that, I'll send my book back, and then just cope.

Karen's benefits amounted to £59.40. Her rent and rates came to £37.40, for which she got a rebate. The phone, electricity and gas bills varied from quarter to quarter, and she couldn't remember what they were. She spent £1.75 a week for the playgroup which her children attended, approximately £31.48 on food, £3.75 on detergents and cleaning materials and a further £8 a week on clothes for her children and herself. Her regular weekly outgoings (excluding rent and rates) amounted to £44.98, which left her with £14.42, out of which had to be found the phone, electricity, gas and other contingency payments. She spent, typically,

Bread	£1.20
Tea	£1.60
Coffee (instant)	£0.93

Sugar	£1.32
Milk	£1.76
Drinking chocolate	£1.06
Coca Cola	£0.47
Cereal	£0.52
Margarine	£0.33
Cakes/biscuits	£2.86
Fresh meat	£10.00
Bacon	£0.75
Sausages	£1.96
Frozen meat	£1.50
Tinned vegetables	£0.52
Frozen vegetables	£2.00
Sweets	£0.38
Cheese	£0.82
Puddings (Instant Whip)	£1.50
Total	£31.48

She never bought fruit or fresh vegetables. Cooking, she readily admitted, posed a problem to her, as did coping with two young children. She therefore took the easier, though perhaps more expensive option of buying tinned and frozen vegetables. Food came to just over half of her income, excluding housing benefit. She fed her boy-friend, and this meant that on average just under £8 a week, or about £1.12 a day, was spent on food per person.

Karen was very friendly with Maggie Thorpe, who lived in the same block of flats. The two had been 'going together' for about six months, sharing their days, their housework chores and their leisure time. (Living, as my grandmother would say 'in each others' pockets'.) In 1983 Maggie was twenty-six and her three children were aged between three and nine. Maggie's husband was a cleaner, 'Well, a day porter, really,' in Cannon Street. Her father was a lorry driver, her mother a cleaner and she was the eldest of a family of five. The flat was in one of the older blocks in Vauxhall, built between the wars, and had two bedrooms. The children shared one, and the parents the other. There was a living room and a kitchen. The flat was sparsely and poorly furnished – the furniture and floor coverings were clearly second-hand and showed the signs of age and overuse. Newspaper was used as lavatory paper. Maggie was born in Vauxhall,

In my nan's flat, downstairs. I moved when I was ten, didn't I? Moved to Bermondsey, then lived with mum for six years, weren't it? Till I left school. Then me nan lost her husband and I lived with her, then I lived with her after I got married and all, didn't I? Till I got this flat.

I left school at sixteen. Got a job with a record company, doing plating when the orders come in. You used to have to get the thing out, put it in a machine and stamp it. Used to do everything – assembling, packing, and then I left there and worked over the NAAFI in Kennington Road, clerical staff. I left there when I was seven months pregnant. Then I had Michelle and went to work for a little while in a baker's over Victoria, part time, then I packed that in, went as a cleaner. That's what I've been doing, on and off. The NAAFI, the Borough, City Road. Offices. It's all right, but it's a bit tiring. Used to go out about half past four and I used to do one at the Borough and then go on to City Road and some nights I never used to get home till about nine, sometimes later than that, according to the buses. But the job expired last February. I'm just waiting now for me mum to ring and say there's another job. She's still supervisor.

Like I say, we lived with me nan when I was married and when we had Michelle there was a confrontation, like. She always used to be moaning. We used to pay towards the electric and the gas. We had our own telly, like, in our own room. And then a row flared up, you know, and me aunt said to me, 'Why don't you write to the council? Or let me write a letter on Mum's behalf,' she said, 'telling them that she's given you a week to get out.' Well then, we wrote that and they offered us a flat, on the ground floor and it was diabolical. There was oxygen things there and it was all burnt out, and wasn't fit for a baby to go in. So my husband mentioned this – and that was how we got our flat. We've been here about eight years now.

We're supposed to be coming out of here soon. But I can't see it. I think we've got another seven years here! You hear people saying, 'Oh, we've got eighteen months,' and then, apparently, they're supposed to have run out of money. I said if we just stick out and wait. I wouldn't mind three bedrooms. I've put in for a three-bedroomed but they said I'm not entitled to one because my girls are not at a certain age, you know? And I had a row with them. My husband wants a house and he wants to move out of London. I don't. I want to sort of stay round here. Quite happy here. The kids know everybody. It's quiet – till the kids come home and it's like Casey's Court!

Like, Tuesday night, Karen went shopping and I had the kids and they was out playing and Michelle's got a coloured friend who lives along the landing. When Karen went home I knocked for her to come in, I said, 'Come on, bed, now.' She said, 'No, I'm not coming in.' You know, once she's out, then that's it. One shout, they play up. Like last night I said 'Right, bed now,' and it was half past seven. 'But can I watch Coronation Street?.' I said, 'You can watch Coronation Street, then go to bed.' 'Yeah, all right,' she said, and they were sitting there – mind you, it was quiet – 'Oh, well, Dallas is on now . . .' I said, 'Bed!' Oh, it's like Casey's Court! Sometimes, if they go to bed late, like if we're round at Karen's sometimes, my husband don't know when to come home, if they go to bed say quarter to one in the morning, then I have trouble with them getting up, like weekdays. I'm not strict – my husband is, to a certain extent. He shouts. I won't let him hit them if I can help it cause he, like, leaves a mark on them, but he'd rather sort of shout and then he gets a bit carried away and keeps on shouting, don't he? I can be if I want to. Like Michelle was cheeky one day – she stuck her two fingers up to me and poked her tongue and I thought there's one way I'll pay her back. She was due to stay at Karen's and I said, 'No, you're coming home', and she sort of didn't know where to look. She thought I was going to give in, but I never.

. . . We drop the kids off and I sort of go up, like, to Karen on a Monday morning. Come back, pick the kids up then we go out. Tuesdays we go shopping. Wednesdays we do all our work. Thursdays I do me washing. We both go out Monday afternoons and Monday nights and the men babysit. And taking it in turns having one of the kids.

It's all right round here. In the summer it's a bit monotonous, like, with the kids outside. They're always fighting and getting into trouble and in the end I just take them out, take them swimming, go up me mum's. I've been going with Karen for about six months and I said in the summer, when the swimming baths open, we'll take the kids. Like, do our work and arrange to meet me sisters and that up my mum's and just go swimming and stay there till we come home. Southwark Park. Round here, see, you've got to pay for all the swimming baths. There you don't have to pay and they've got like a big one for all the grown-ups and a small one like for the kids. We have a laugh. We take sandwiches and drinks, have a right laugh.

Maggie's nan was

taken ill where she wasn't cooking for herself. She's sixty-eight and I decided, I said to me husband about it, I said, 'She's not eating,' I said, 'If we give her so much a week, if we have the meals with her, then we know then that she's eating.'

This arrangement continued, with her nan cooking the main meal of the day, even when Maggie's husband was out of work and

he used to get his money, and we used to be down me nan's, like, having meals. We used to pay her, and then I had me family allowance and I was doing cleaning then. I shouldn't have been, but I was. Me nan helped then.

Maggie's husband brought home approximately £70 a week, though it varied 'over-time wise'. The family allowance of £17.55 brought the income to £87.55, of which the outgoings were:

Rent and rates	£19.72
Husband's bus fares	£7.50
School dinners, etc.	£5.20
Entertainment	£6.00
Food and cleaning materials	£25
Total	£63.42
Surplus	£24.13

From the surplus would need to be found money for the quarterly gas and electricity bills (which varied), clothing, and annual payments such as that for the television licence. Maggie did not have a telephone. Because the food and cooking was shared with her nan it was difficult for her to detail her expenditure precisely, but in a typical week she bought:

Bread	£1.48
Tea	£0.65
Coffee (instant)	£0.95
Sugar	£0.46½
Cocoa	£0.45
Coca Cola	£0.25
Cereal	£0.60
Jam/marmalade	£0.39½
Butter	£0.55½
Margarine	£0.30
Cakes/biscuits	£0.15½
Fresh meat	£2.40
Bacon	£1.35
Sausages	£0.56

Ham	£0.62
Frozen beefburgers	£0.55
Fish (frozen)	£0.98
Fish and chips	£1.08
Vegetables (fresh)	£0.54
Fruit	£2.00
Sweets	£0.70
Cheese	£0.64
Rice	£0.28
Total	£17.95

Although fish and some meat was bought frozen, no vegetables were. Frozen meat and fish compares favourably in price with fresh produce, unlike frozen vegetables. This was the typical week's menu she detailed (although it did not tally with the budget she gave):

Sunday	Breakfast:	eggs, bacon, tomatoes
	Dinner:	meat, baked potatoes, vegetables, batter pudding
	Tea:	fruit, custard cakes
Monday	Breakfast:	toast, jam, tea
	Dinner:	sausages, potatoes, vegetables, tea
	Tea:	egg on toast
Tuesday	Breakfast:	cereal, tea
	Dinner:	snack sandwich
	Tea:	shepherd's pie, vegetables, tea
Wednesday	Breakfast:	toast, jam, tea
	Dinner:	snack
	Tea:	fish fingers, chips, vegetables, tea
Thursday	Breakfast:	cereal, tea
	Dinner:	snack
	Tea:	pie, potatoes, vegetables, tea

Friday   Breakfast: egg, toast, tea
                   Dinner: snack
                   Tea: pork, baked potatoes,
                               vegetables, tea

Saturday   Breakfast: cereal, tea
                   Dinner: snack
                   Tea: braised lamb, potatoes,
                               vegetables, tea

Rent amounted to nearly one-quarter of the income and food to just over one-third. Approximately £4.50 a week or 64p a day was spent on food per person.

In 1984 Debbie Stebbings was twenty-eight, and her daughter was ten. She had lived all her life in and around Kennington, and now lives in Kennington Lane. She works as a baby-minder.

My mum didn't know I was pregnant till the day I had her. For the simple fact that I've always been big. The father of Carol is married anyway, I knew this, and I didn't spend an awful lot of time at home, I spent it at my friend's house. It sounds stupid now, but I just used to come home of a night, go straight to me room and put me nightie and me dressing gown on, and she couldn't see then. I mean . . . it was the fact that I could hide it, it was unnoticeable. And I just happened to be home actually the morning that me water broke. I can visualise it now! We was living in Kennington Road, and my sister must have been nine and my brother was eight and we only had two bedrooms and my mum, dad, my brother and sister were all in the same bedroom and I had my own bedroom, being older. And I got up at seven o'clock in the morning to go to the toilet and me water broke, and I went running into the bedroom and I said, 'I know I should have told you before,' I said, 'but I'm having a baby and me water's just broke.' And that is just the exact words that came out, and her reaction was, 'Oh, quick, George, go and phone the ambulance.'

I realise now that it was very foolish – I could have done myself harm and I could have done the baby harm. But at the time I didn't think. I mean, only eighteen when I had her. I was seventeen when I fell pregnant. She was born a breech, which is something they said could have been avoided had I of been under constant check. I didn't have a thing – I didn't have a nappy, a nappy pin, I didn't have a thing. And when I came out, I had everything. I mean, literally, they'd all gone out and brought brand new – the pram, the cot, the clothes, the whole lot. The whole family had been out and brought the whole lot.

I lived at home afterwards, with her. Mum looked after Carol when I went back to work. It was only when she got to about eighteen months that it was getting a bit too much for her and she was trying to run a business as well, and she couldn't cope with both, that I got her put into an all-day nursery. We continued like that until she was about three and a half and things were rough at home, the friction was . . . the atmosphere was terrible. And we had one big bust-up on the Thursday night and I took her and went to stay to my friend's house, then Friday morning I went down the Homeless at Brixton and said that I'd had this great big argument and they said that because she hadn't thrown me out there was nothing they could do! So I stood the ground. I mean, I knew this was ridiculous and I'd been on the council list since she'd been born and obviously, living with them and having adequate room, they'd not bothered to rehouse me. They said my brother could have slept with my mum and dad till he was ten, and my sister likewise but I stood my ground.

So they sent me to a bed and breakfast hotel at Crystal Palace which was marvellous. Admittedly you only had one room but I had a double bed for myself and Carol and we had a sink in the room and we had our own television and we had a bathroom and toilet outside that door and then upstairs on another landing was the communal kitchen, where there was a fridge, a washing machine, where you could just cook whenever you wanted. And because I was out at work all day and Carol was at the nursery all day long, it wasn't too bad to put up with.

I moved in there in September and was offered my first flat in Kennington in May, which I accepted. The flat itself wasn't bad, it was a two-bedroomed, ground floor and semi-basement, but I wasn't happy there and I moved in there in May and I got an exchange to this flat in February. I've been here seven years . . .

I've lived with Tom for seven years. I met him actually just as I moved in. I had a house-warming party and I met him. And we've been together ever since. I was on social security from the Christmas till about October that year, until we finally lived together. Social wasn't bad, I managed to get a little part-time job round the corner which fitted in . . . but it was tough. I'd always worked and always had more. It wasn't the fact that the money was so low, it was the fact that I was used to more and it was just a case of adapting to a lower wage from what you was on. Plus the fact of being home all day long which I wasn't happy with, I didn't enjoy being home all day long . . .

Her boy-friend is a self-employed carpenter.

He made that telly cabinet and he made Carol's bed – he's a cabinet-maker really and he's doing very, very well. Really and truly, I've never had it as good as what I'm having it now. When I first lived with Tom my mum didn't like it. She'll bring out some snidey remark, even now. I mean, I might get something new and she'll come up and say, 'Oh, who bought that?' All I'll say, 'Tom bought it.' And she'll say 'He's entitled to, he shares your flat, and he shares your bed.' And this is her attitude to it, not that we live as a pair and all right, the tenancy is in my name, but it doesn't mean that it's my flat . . .

. . . I've always been in close contact with the nursery which is across the road and we used to pop in there of a morning and the mums used to have a chat upstairs in one room and the kids used to play downstairs and that, and there was a lady over there who'd just had a baby and she said would I consider looking after it. I love babies and I said, well, yeah. And I started off with him. I stuck with him for ages and ages, then I got another and once I had two to look after, I applied and got registered.

I've got three now. By about 5.15 there's no one. Tom doesn't get in till about 7.15 so it gives me ample time to clear up and get dinner ready before he does come home. Plus I'm still here in the holidays when Carol's off school, you know? Sometimes she moans a bit because we can't go where she wants to go in the holidays because it means dragging all the kids with us.

The only time I find it a bit restricting is if I want to go anywhere. You haven't literally got five minutes when you haven't got one kid – you've always got someone about. But as I say, I enjoy it. I can't do it for the money – you get 50p an hour! And food and everything else has got to come out of that, so it's not a lot, really, not when you take out what you spend. You don't get any paid holiday, and if a child's off sick for a couple of days, they don't pay me for those two days, or if I was off sick – which isn't very often – but if I was off sick then I wouldn't get paid for them days. If I was employed I would get sick pay, holiday pay.

I don't believe in childminding, even though I do it. I don't believe in it. I look at it this way, I had to go back to work because I was on my own. But if you are a married couple, then I think the place should be with the children.

As a registered childminder, Debbie earned between £50 and £55 per week. The family allowance amounted to £6.50 and their total family income, with Tom's earnings, was between £300 and £350 per week. They regularly afforded an annual holiday in Jersey, and spent a considerable amount on entertainment. The flat had two bedrooms and was in one of the newer blocks. It was light, airy and very clean, with new furniture and furnishings. Tom had made some of the furniture, as well as the fitted units, and money was clearly spent on keeping the flat smart and modern. Carol's room for instance, contained a small four-poster bed with curtains and drapes to match. Their total weekly outgoings were as follows.

Rent and rates	£30.00
Electricity	£6.00
Gas	£3.50
Telephone	£4.00
Boy-friend's travel fares	£27.00
Hire purchase	£10.00
Clothes	£10–£15.00
School dinners, etc.	£3.50
Entertainment	£20–£30.00
Detergents, cleaning materials	£5.00
Food	£40–£50.00
Total	£159–184

A typical weekly shop would buy:

Bread	£2.00
Tea	£3.00
Milk	£4.50
Cocoa	£1.75
Coca Cola/squash	£1.00
Butter	£1.00
Margarine	£0.82
Cakes/biscuits	£1.50
Fresh meat	£10–£15.00
Bacon	£1.50
Sausages	£1.00
Cooked meats	£1.00
Frozen meat meals	£2.50
Vegetables (fresh)	£2.00
Fruit	£2.00
Sweets	£2.00
Cheese	£1.00
Rice/pasta	£0.50
Total	£39.07–£44.07

Debbie liked cooking and detailed the family menu for a typical week as follows.

Sunday	Breakfast:	eggs, bacon, toast, tomatoes
	Dinner:	joint or chicken, vegetables, potatoes
	Tea:	sandwich from left-over roast
Monday	Breakfast:	nil
	Dinner:	beans on toast
	Tea:	fish fingers, chips, peas, bread
Tuesday	Breakfast:	nil
	Dinner:	scrambled eggs and spaghetti
	Tea:	shepherd's pie, chips and peas
Wednesday	Breakfast:	nil
	Dinner:	sausages and chips
	Tea:	Ham and egg pie, chips, peas
Thursday	Breakfast:	nil
	Dinner:	cheese on toast
	Tea:	corned beef, hash, cabbage
Friday	Breakfast:	nil
	Dinner:	ham and egg, chips
	Tea:	steak, mushrooms, chips, tomatoes
Saturday	Breakfast:	eggs, bacon, tomatoes, toast
	Dinner:	jacket potatoes with cheese
	Tea:	take-away Chinese or Indian meal

Rent amounted to about one-tenth of the income and food to about one-sixth. It is difficult to calculate precisely how much was spent on food per person since the food budget included a main meal for the children in her charge. This meal, as she pointed out, was a good meal, cooked by herself. But on average, about £12 a week was spent on food per person, or £1.70 a day.

Deirdre Patel was thirty-six in 1987. She had emigrated from Ireland when she was fifteen. She had been brought up there by her grandfather who

> . . . was very protective. He wouldn't let me out a lot with friends and that. I used to sneak out the windows at night, go to the dances. And then next day he'd have a go at me. He used to like his drink, me grandad . . . and he always had money, he always backed the horses, loved the horses. He loved me, but one day he went to hit me and he sort of fell forward and I jumped out of the way . . . When he come home he'd be drunk, so each time he come home drunk this is what I done – maybe I shouldn't be telling you – I used to nick his money out of his pockets. I did! That's terrible! Then I wait till I had my fill, and one day I said to him, 'I'm going away' and he said, 'Where?' I said 'I've written to my aunt who lives in Black Prince Road and she said I ought to come to her.' I don't think I had any sense, because I left and I had 5s. [25p] in my pocket. I came over on the boat and somebody from Carlow was leaving as well that day. We were on the boat together. When we got to Victoria, his brother was supposed to meet him and never turned up. He had no money. My aunt turned up, with my uncle. And I felt sorry for him. Michael was his name, and I remember giving him half a crown [12½p] . . .
>
> So I stayed with my aunt. She's better than my own mother. She always gives the children a rig-out at Christmas and, like, when it's Mother's Day I always buy her a bunch of flowers. She's great. I went to work in a children's hospital in the Borough, as a maid, lived in. I loved it there. Waiting, on the tables, the doctors and nurses one side and at the end, the sisters. You'd have to serve them properly, from the left. We done silly things, little things that you can look back on now and have a laugh about it. But the forewoman, she was horrible. She kept annoying the staff. I had a friend there,

Noreen, Irish girl, and she got the sack. She wasn't doing her work properly. Noreen was lazy. And I said 'I'm leaving.' I did.

Then I worked for a greengrocer, and he let me have two rooms above the shop and every dinner-time this bloke used to go by, used to walk up and down. He'd just say 'Hallo' – then he just asked me out. Started going out with him and then he said to me one day not to get serious, we should cool it, and I said, 'All right.' But I was really fond of him at the time. We did for about a month, and then we got back together. And that was it. Got married in a registry office. His mother seemed all right at the time, but she never appreciated me. I think the family were jealous that he got married to a white girl. Then he left me when my eldest was a year and eleven months and I was pregnant again. We used to argue a lot and his mum interfered. One day he just got me and said, 'I'm going back to Mum's.' The next thing I knew he was gone to Zaïre, to his relations, and I wrote a letter and kept saying to him, 'Have me back.' And me, like a silly old devil, I went and sold everything up and went after him. I'd never been abroad in my life, never been on a plane nor nothing, and I went five thousand miles . . .

Pregnant. And I had Jalal. Over there they mostly speak French and I can't speak French. I was standing there, at the airport, with a belly, and Jalal and two suitcases. I did, really did. And then he turned up, an hour late. We seemed to get on all right. Then off he went to Nigeria – he had an auntie there.

I went with him. Then the auntie was moving back to Kenya and we came back here, on the plane, not even talking to each other. We hadn't spoken for about a month. And he said, 'As soon as I get back to London I'm leaving you.' And I kept crying and begging and saying, 'Don't leave me, don't leave me.' I was very, very stupid. I said, 'Got no money.' I'd sold up everything I had to get the fare to go over there. But he took me by taxi and signed me in to a room in Victoria for the night. I said, 'Aren't you staying the night?' And he said,

'No.' I said, 'I'm not staying here on me own.' And he said, 'Well, I don't want you.'

I started screaming. I said to the girl in the hotel, 'Give me back the money' and I just walked out of the door. I'd had to borrow a coat even because all me clothes I'd given away. Had a belly out here and my little boy in the pushchair and I walked around. This was eleven o'clock at night and I was crying at my aunt's door and she said, 'Oh, my God, whatever's the matter with you?' She took me in and I was there for about four days and she said, 'You're going to have to go to the social and you're going to have to go up to Homeless Families and tell them.' They put me in a place in Brixton, and I was there one year and one month. I had my second child. She came at eight months, in Lambeth Hospital. I came out of there and I didn't have a cot even for her to sleep in. She slept in a bath. They gave me a double bed. I made it look – well, you do – you make it look pretty. There was a little cooker in there, but it was small. There was a wardrobe in it, there was a bed, a table and chairs. I used to cry at night and think, 'Why is he doing it to me, why?' I used to feel sorry for myself. I don't think I was grown-up enough.

I used to see people coming and going and getting places. They offered me three places and I refused them, they were terrible. I got to the stage that one bloke turned round and said, 'We'll evict you from Homeless Families,' and a chap there said, 'They won't do it to you. They're only frightening you to make you take a place.' I waited, and then was offered a place. And I came and seen it, and I took it. When I took this place it was – oh God! It was the people in it before me, they just left, left all the bills – it was so dirty here, it was unbelievable. I walked in the room and I said, 'This is my own place.' But it was filthy, there was even mess on the walls, the toilet. But I thought, gradually, gradually . . . I moved in here with nothing. Honest to God. Somebody gave me a bed, my aunt came over with pillows and blankets. We was in here with just a bed upstairs and TV. And then social came and gave me a table and chairs, and gave me money for lino, but I waited and tried to save up and bought me carpet, and then slowly, slowly . . . I've done a lot to it, I learnt to do things myself.

Five years I never went out with anybody. I used to keep thinking of my husband. I do love their dad. He's never given my kids a penny, and he's never written to them. He never sent them a card, nothing. But his brother, he always give me a bit of money, even if it was a fiver. And he came one day with his friend [who] said to me could he take me out. And then one night he ended up . . . you know, so I did and . . . this. And when I told him he didn't want to know. I said, 'All right then, you don't want to know, but do me one favour. Come and be at the hospital with me, visit me every night.' Because I had my second on my own and it was terrible. You just felt, alone.

Then when she was born, he was over the moon. I cared about him a lot, but I didn't love him. She was born and he was up every night, big bunch of flowers, and his mother and father turned up. Then one day he came and said, 'I don't care about you any more. It must have been infatuation.' Well, I just went completely berserk. I went so funny. I broke all my plants up – I love plants – and everything. And he went away . . . to work in Nigeria. Twice in her four years he sent money, and he sent her two little rings once as well. I suppose he does love her in his own way. That's it. Haven't heard from him since.

Her grandparents, for a whole year they didn't see her. And then once the grandad came. He was crying and he said, 'You broke our hearts.' And I'm a right old idiot, softy, and he was hugging her and then I got on the phone and I said, 'If you want to have her for the weekend you can.' Oh, you know, when they came and collected her they were all over me. You'd never believe it. And then they wanted to take her to Canada and I wouldn't let them. You see, my husband's mother was going to see their dad, last year, and take my eldest with her. Everything was arranged and I had a phone call. Even now I don't know . . . the call was anonymous, saying to me that I was sending him on a holiday and – how did they put it? – they admired me for bringing the kids up on my own, but beware of his mother, because she was going to leave my son over there with his dad. I asked the health visitor's advice, went over to the law centre . . . I didn't let him go.

I have a little job, cleaning. I get in a routine. When the summer comes, I'll take them out, for walks, we take a little picnic, Crystal Palace or something like that. But in the winter you can't. It's a depressing time in the winter. Maybe other people can't cope, so I suppose I'm lucky. In that sense, I used my loaf. I'd just like to have enough, I would, for a rainy day, that I wouldn't have to, wait till your family allowance comes in to buy something. I wouldn't like to be rich or anything like that . . .

Deirdre continued working as a cleaner and met, through her work, the area manager of a cleaning firm with whom she began a relationship and now lives. She has also had a child by him, and they were rehoused in a three-bedroomed council house in Kennington. It was a three-storey terraced Victorian house that, in 1913, may well have housed three or more families. The house had been rehabilitated by the council but her boy-friend, a keen and talented DIY enthusiast, improved it further with the installation of double glazing – a necessity for the house fronts one of the busier main roads. The house was clean and cosy and both partners had made considerable effort to improve it. The bathroom had its fitments enclosed in mahogany panelling and care had been taken to maintain the 'period' qualities of the house through the choice of decoration. Her partner's income was approximately £600 a month, out of which he paid £60 in maintenance for a child by his previous marriage. Deirdre still worked as a cleaner and earned, net, £29 per week. The family allowance came to £116 per month. Their weekly income was approximately £193. Their weekly outgoings were as follows:

Rent and rates	£29.00
Electricity	£4.40(£53 per quarter)
Gas	£3.40(£41 per quarter)
Telephone	£5 (£60 per quarter)
Bus fares	£6.60
Children's clothes	£5.00,mainly from Freeman's catalogue
Clothes for mother	£1.00
Personal things, cosmetics, etc:	£2.50
School dinners	£15.00
Children's extras	£1.00
Entertainment	£1.00(very occasional, perhaps twice a year when £22 would be spent on a night out)
Cleaning materials	£2.50(the man brings home most of the household cleaning materials)
Food	£63.89
Cigarettes (for the man)	£10.50
Total	£150.79

Compared with many families Deirdre's appeared well off, with just over £42 per week in hand. Out of this they were able to make occasional savings. Her partner had a car for his work, but petrol used for domestic consumption had to be paid out of surplus. Money for the father's clothes had also to be found – and school uniform for the eldest child, which cost £160. The eldest son does not go to school locally: 'No way, not round here. I fought hard to get him into Westminster College. I'll do the same for the others, too, when they're older.' The baby's food and disposable nappies – 'she's the big expense' – cost between £11 and £12 per week.

Shopping was done at the large Sainsbury's once every two weeks, and in the market for 'bits and bobs'. Her boy-friend helped her with the large shop at Sainsbury's, but other than that she walked to the market with the baby in her buggy. On average, the food for this family of six was as follows:

Bread	£3.00
Tea	£1.20
Coffee (instant)	£0.80
Sugar	£1.20
Milk	£4.00
Soft drinks	£2.80
Alcohol (bottle of wine/beer)	£1.50
Cereal	£1.40
Peanut butter/chocolate spread	£0.80
Butter	£0.70
Cakes/biscuits	£1.80
Frozen meat, bought in bulk	£15.00
Bacon	£2.00
Sausages	£1.40
Cooked meats (ham)	£1.00
Frozen meals, burgers, cod steaks	£8.00
Vegetables (fresh and tinned)	£6.00
Fruit	£4.00
Sweets	£1.00
Cheese	£1.50
Puddings/yogurt	£2.99
Rice/pasta	£1.80
Total	£63.89

In the summer, they often took a trip out of London to pick their own fruit and vegetables. Once petrol had been added this did not significantly reduce the cost of the fruit, but it provided an outing. Again, the food prepared was traditional.

The Sunday joint cost about £5 and provided a main meal, and sandwiches in the evening. Other than that it was 'chips, eggs and ham, or gammon steaks, boiled potatoes and beans, or beefburgers and chips, or chicken drumsticks, potatoes and vegetables, or fish fingers, pies, the usual . . .'

The rent consumed approximately one-sixth of the income, and food approximately one-third. The baby was budgeted separately, so just under £13 a week, or £1.80 a day, was spent on food per person.

Tenacity, mobility, standing up for rights, 'pestering' – however diverse the life histories, these were the themes which united them. They found echoes elsewhere. Karen Howard for instance has:

> . . . two bedrooms here, but one room's too cold. I told the council that. They say it's condensation. 'Leave your windows open.' Leave your windows open?! With a baby? I phones up the council and said, 'There's water on my wall.' See, Mum has one room, so I've got to sleep in the front room with the cot, and me and Mark sleep on the settee. The man from the council said, 'No.' I said, 'Yeah.' He came round, he said, 'Oh, leave your windows open and that water will go.' I said, 'So my baby's got to catch pneumonia before you do something? No way! *You* live here!'
>
> I went up there the other day. I gave them a piece of my mind. It's all right for them, see, they've got nice houses. They don't care if you're living in an old scum dump. I said it to them and all. I said, 'Bet you've got a lovely central heating place, no worries about condensation on the windows and walls.' They didn't answer me . . . We're still waiting. I used to pester the daylights out of them.

Judy Chalmers, who was rehoused in Peckham, which she hated, kept 'pestering the council and finally they moved me back into this block, about two or three doors away from my mother.'

Sometimes it is necessary to deviate, to find extra income

through the job market often controlled by women. Thus cleaning jobs require no formal application, no skills. But to get one involves entering a network – an aunt (as in Deirdre's case), a mother (like Maggie's), a neighbour or a friend who can pass out and parcel the work. As Jackie Ball described,

> There's a sort of network among them. I think the firms do well out of that because they never have to advertise for vacancies, they've only got to say that we need a new cleaner and the word will go out on the network and somebody will appear. You put the word out on the network, no questions asked type thing.

No questions asked meant being 'in the know'. Judy, for instance, through her family and her network in the market, was never short of bulk supplies of coffee and other goods. Deirdre got her cleaning materials free. Debbie had her furniture made. Both Greta and Deirdre got their flats, partly by persistence, partly by nurturing a relationship with their housing officer. No sound of dropsy falling, but echoes perhaps of knowing the landlord well enough to negotiate, as Sal Beckford could do in the 1930s,

> . . . a little place, little flat going next door. There was two rooms on the level. They was 18s. [90p] a week. So I said to the caretaker, 'Could I have them rooms?' He said, you'll have to move in by Monday (then) you won't pay no extra rent. We'll carry on with your 16s. [80p] . . .

And some reminders of Sue Dexter, who, in 1936, when she was first married and was

> . . . living on about 25s. [£1.25]. What could you do? We were paying 12s. 6d. [12½p] a week rent in one room . . . He was an errand boy, and he used to bring home jars of caviare and tins of *petits pois* peas. So he'd eat the caviare, and I'd eat the peas and maybe a tin of fruit now and again . . . And this is how we were living.

Maud Pember Reeves first drew attention to the resourcefulness and resilience of the women in North Lambeth. In tracing the lives of their successors it is these qualities, above all, that I too have found, and have sought to explore.

Bibliography

Books

Brian Abel-Smith and Peter Townsend, *The Poor and the Poorest*, Bell & Sons, London, 1965.

C. Booth, *Labour and Life of the People*, Vol. II, London, 1891.

Michael Chanon, *The Dream That Kicks*, Routledge & Kegan Paul, London, 1980.

J. Clarke, C. Critcher, R. Johnson, *Working Class Culture: Studies in History and Theory*, Hutchinson, London, 1979.

Cynthia Cockburn, *The Local State*, Pluto Press, London, 1978.

D. Donnison, *The Politics of Poverty*, Martin Robertson & Co., Oxford, 1982.

Diana Gittins, *The Family in Question*, Macmillan, London, 1985.

J. Greve et al., *Homelessness in London*, Scottish Academic Press, Edinburgh, 1971.

P. G. Hall, *The Industries of London Since 1861*, Hutchinson, London, 1962.

Judy Hillman, *Planning for London*, Penguin, Harmondsworth, 1971.

Home Sweet Home: Housing Designed by the LCC and GLC Architects 1888–1975, London Architectural Monographs, Academy Editions, London, 1976.

Stuart MacLure, *One Hundred Years of London Education 1870–1970*, Allen Lane, London, 1970.

Honor Marshall, *Twilight London: A Study in Degradation*, Vision Press, London, 1971.

Dennis Marsden, *Mothers Alone*, Allen Lane, London, 1969.

J. E. Martin, *Greater London: An Industrial Geography*, Bell & Sons, London, 1966.

Doreen Massey and John Allen (eds.), *Geography Matters!* Cambridge University Press, Cambridge, 1984.

Matrix, *Making Space: Women and the Man Made Environment*, Pluto Press, London, 1984.

Andrew Mearns, *The Bitter Cry of Outcast London*, Leicester

University Press, Leicester, 1970.

New Survey of London Life and Labour, vols. V, VI, IX, London, 1934.

Alexander Paterson, *Across the Bridges*, Edward Arnold, London, 1911.

Maud Pember Reeves, *Round About a Pound a Week*, Virago, London, 1979.

Janet Roebuck, *Urban Development in 19th Century London*, Phillimore & Co., Chichester, 1979.

David Rubinstein, *School Attendance in London 1870–1904*, Occasional Papers in Economic and Social History, no. 1, University of Hull, 1969.

Michael Rutter and Nicola Madge, *Cycles of Deprivation*, Heinemann, London, 1976.

Hugh Quigley and Ismay Goldie, *Housing and Slum Clearance in London*, Methuen, London, 1934.

Eliot Slater and Moya Woodside, *Patterns of Marriage*, Cassell, London, 1951.

Social Services in North Lambeth and Kennington: A Study for the Lady Margaret Hall Settlement, Oxford University Press, Oxford, 1939.

Mark Swenarton, *Homes Fit For Heroes*, Heinemann, London, 1981.

Nicholas Taylor, *The Village in the City*, Temple Smith, London, 1973.

Melanie Tebbutt, *Making Ends Meet*, Methuen, London, 1984.

R. M. Titmuss, *Income Distribution and Social Change*, Allen & Unwin, London, 1962.

Peter Townsend, *Poverty in the United Kingdom*, Penguin, Harmondsworth, 1979.

Peter Townsend (ed.), *The Concept of Poverty*, Heinemann, London, 1970.

D. Wedderburn (ed.), *Poverty, Inequality and Class Structure*, Cambridge University Press, Cambridge, 1974.

Elizabeth Wilson, *Women and the Welfare State*, Tavistock, London, 1977.

Anthony Wohl, *The Eternal Slum*, Edward Arnold, London, 1977.

Articles

N. Cameron, 'The Growth of London School Children 1904–1966: An Analysis of Secular Trend and Intra-county Variations', *Annals of Human Biology*, vol. 6, no. 6, 1979.

A. R. Garman, S. Chinn and R. Rona, 'Comparative Growth of

Primary School Children From One and Two Parent Families', *Archives of Disease in Childhood*, 57, 1982.

Charles Gatliff, 'On Improved Dwellings and their Beneficial Effect on Health and Morals with Suggestions for their Extension', *Journal of the Statistical Society of London*, XXXVIII, March, 1975.

The Housing Journal, selected issues, 1900–1920.

Chris Pond and Louie Burghes, 'The Rising Tide of Deprivation', *New Society*, 18 April 1986.

R. Rona and S. Chinn, 'National Study of Health and Growth: Nutritional Surveillance of Primary School Children from 1972–1981 With Special Reference to Unemployment and Social Class', *Annals of Human Biology*, vol. II, no. 1, 1984.

R. J. Rona, S. Chinn, A. M. Smith, 'School Meals and Rate of Growth of Primary Schoolchildren', *Journal of Epidemiology and Community Health*, no. 37, 1983.

R. J. Rona, A. V. Swan, D. G. Altman, 'Social Factors in Height of Primary School Children in England and Scotland', *Journal of Epidemiology and Community Medicine*, no. 32, 1978.

A. Smith, S. Chinn, R. Rona, 'Social Factors and Height Gain of Primary Schoolchildren in England and Scotland', *Annals of Human Biology*, 7, 1980.

South London Press (various years).

Titbits, selected issues, 1932–1939.

Weldon's Home Dressmaker, selected issues, 1931–1939.

Woman, selected issues, 1937–1939.

Woman's Own, selected issues, 1932–1939.

Woman's Weekly, selected issues, 1928–1939.

Reports

Behavioural Science Unit and an Interdepartmental Working Party, *The Relationship between the GLC Housing Department, its Tenants and the Public*, GLC Research Memorandum RM 503, 1977.

Birth Statistics Historical Series, 1837–1983, FMI, no. 13, HMSO.

Borough of Lambeth, *Annual Report of the Medical Officer of Health*, 1901–1957.

H. C. Corry-Mann, 'Diets for Boys During the School Age', *Medical Research Council Special Report*, series no. 105, HMSO, 1928.

County of London Plan, 1943.

General Lying-In Hospital, Medical Committee Minute Books 1907–1949, Ladies' Committee Minute Books 1907–1939,

Matron's Weekly Reports 1881–1926, Annual Reports.

Greater London Council, *The London Industrial Strategy*, 1985.

Inner London Education Authority, *School Health Service Reports*, 1965–1968.

Inner London: Policies for Dispersal and Balance, HMSO, 1977.

Lady Margaret Hall Settlement, *Report*, April 1913–1914.

Lambeth Archives IV/108, IV/56/4 D81508 (Hayles & Walcot Charities).

Lambeth Board of Guardians, Ladies' Committee Signed Minutes 1903–1910, Settlement Examinations, Orders of Removal Inwards, Register of Orders of Removal and Adjudication Inwards 1850–1927, Orders of Removal Outwards 1834–1930, Admission and Discharge Registers, Workhouse, Renfrew Road 1868–1919.

Lambeth Distress Committee, *Unemployed Workman Act*, 1907.

Lambeth Borough Council, *Minutes of Housing Committee*, 4 June 1947.

Lambeth Borough Council, *Minutes of Public Health Committee*, 11 February 1946.

Lambeth Borough Council, *Report of Special Committee on London Planning*, Council Minutes, 21 October 1947.

Lambeth Housing Movement, *Lambeth Housing Ltd*, 1934.

Lambeth Official Guide, 1948.

Lambeth Hospital, Medical Officer's Report Book.

Lambeth Vestry and Metropolitan Borough Annual Reports, selected years.

Local Authority Vital Statistics, series VS no. 1, OPCS, 1974.

Local Authority Vital Statistics, series VS no. 7, OPCS, 1980.

London Borough of Lambeth, *1981 Census: Ward Profiles*, RM23, 1981.

London Borough of Lambeth, *Estate Profiles: 1981 Census Results*.

London Borough of Lambeth, *Lambeth Analysis of Employment Change at the Individual Firm Level 1978–83*.

London Borough of Lambeth, *Results of the 1978/79 Land Use and Employment Survey for Lambeth*, RM19.

London Borough of Lambeth, *Waterloo District Plan*, 1977.

London Borough of Lambeth, *Into the Seventies: London Borough of Lambeth Housing Committee, a Review of the Demand, Supply and Costs, 1969*.

London County Council, *London Statistics*, vol. XXXVI, 1931–32.

London County Council, *Minutes of Housing Committee and Public Health*, 1947.

London County Council, *Report by School Medical Officer on the Average Height and Weights of Elementary School Children in the County of London*, 1938.

London County Council, *Report on the Heights and Weights of School Pupils in the County of London*, 1959.

Minutes of the London County Council, 1933–1957.

Maternity Alliance, *Born Unequal*, 1985.

Mortality Statistics, series DH5 no. 1, OPCS, 1974.

Mortality Statistics, series DH5 no. 7, OPCS, 1980.

Mortality Statistics: Childhood, series DH3 no. 1, OPCS, 1974.

Mortality Statistics: Childhood, series DH3 no. 8, OPCS, 1980.

Mortality Statistics: Perinatal and Infant: Social and Biological Factors, series DH3 no. 18, OPCS, 1985.

National Association for Maternity and Child Welfare, *Report of Annual Conference on Maternity and Child Welfare*, 1951.

'One Parent Family Housing'. The response of the National Council for One-parent Families to the Government's Consultative Document on Housing Policy, February 1978.

Population and Vital Statistics: Local and Health Authority Area Summary series VS no. 12, PPI no. 8, OPCS, 1985.

Post Office, *London Directory*, 1931.

The Registrar General's Statistical Review for England and Wales, 1933 (HMSO, 1935), 1936 (HMSO, 1938), 1946 (HMSO, 1948), 1951 (HMSO, 1954), 1961, parts II and III (HMSO, 1964), 1971, part II (HMSO, 1973).

Reports of the Mothers' Institute, Joanna Street, Lambeth ('Barley Mow'), 1914–1965.

Royal Waterloo Hospital, *Board Minutes Books*.

St Thomas's Hospital Reports, Minutes of Almoners' Committee 1907–1947.

St Thomas's Hospital Reports, new series, 'Report of the Obstetrical Department', 1911–1930.

Margaret Whitehead, *The Health Divide*, Health Education Council, 1987.

Index